FRANCE PAGAN?

FRANCE PAGAN?

The Mission of Abbé Godin

MAISIE WARD

With a Foreword by

HIS EMINENCE CARDINAL GRIFFIN

NEW YORK
SHEED AND WARD
1949

MANUFACTURED
IN THE UNITED STATES OF AMERICA

FOREWORD

THIS book makes most fascinating reading. It shows the efforts made by the Church in France, under the able guidance of His Eminence Cardinal Suhard, to meet new problems with new methods. It is the record of the courage and enterprise of a small band of priests to win the workers to Christ. The difficulties and failures of the mission are exposed with great candour; and the safeguards in this vastly important experiment are set out with admirable clarity. On the other hand, we learn of the tremendous success which must inevitably follow any work so fired with the love of God and carried through in a manner so utterly regardless of the sacrifices which missionary labours demand.

It is still an open question whether the apostolate for the worker is the more satisfactorily fulfilled by the priest's undertaking factory work. But to me this does not seem an essential part of the apostolate. What is important is that the priest should know his people intimately so that he may be able to guide and help them in their daily lives, in the family, in factory and workshop, in their work and in their recreation. Parish visiting, which in this country is, thank God, of custom and obligation, is the first step in obtaining this necessary knowledge. The work of the priest for the family is greatly emphasised in this book.

We have much to learn from studying this missionary movement in France: a deep sympathy with others and an abounding generosity in the service of our Divine Master; a knowledge that our goal can only be attained by prayer, work and penance. For these reasons I warmly welcome this book.

ARCHBISHOP'S HOUSE,   ✠ BERNARD CARDINAL GRIFFIN
WESTMINSTER,   Archbishop of Westminster
LONDON, S.W.1   15th November 1948

v

INTRODUCTION

READING *France, Pays de Mission ?* made me feel at once the vital importance of its being known to the English-speaking world and the impossibility of merely a straight translation. There were many pages of area statistics and comparisons that would be of little interest outside France, while matter of great general interest was printed in small type or relegated to a footnote. There were so many repetitions that I almost fancied I must have been dreaming and have read the same passage over and over again. Then, too, a subject would be started, abandoned, returned to, almost as though notes were being taken. Finally I realised that this was exactly the case. Two men had written the book and of those two the leading spirit was a man who wrote all he wrote by way of notes—scratched in the small hours when he was half asleep after a twenty-hour day or jotted down between pressing engagements. Clearly if the book were to carry its message some omissions and adaptations must be made, and I gained permission from the publishers to make them. Thus adapted, *France, Pays de Mission ?* appears as Part II of the present book. The chapter and section numberings do not correspond with the original.

And then the man himself began to grow on me—with something of the fascination, the personal magnetism he had for his disciples, for the boys and girls and young couples whom he depicted so vividly and in whose lives he lived so wholeheartedly. This man was surely even more interesting than the book he had written. And so it proved. From his life by Canon Glorieux, from the *Témoignages* of the *Editions Ouvrières*, from men who had known him I drew the sketch which, incomplete though it be, will, I hope, do something to introduce a most extraordinary personality. I have made the sketch of Abbé Godin Part I of this book.

The difficulty of conveying the atmosphere of the Paris slums and of this priest who lived in them is obvious. I am very grateful to Father Eugene Langdale for what he describes as " putting in the swear words ". But I have not on the whole attempted to put the French slang into English slang, especially as I would have had to put it also into American slang! And slang changes so quickly. It has usually seemed better to indicate it rather than to attempt a translation. One thing which I found very colourful is the tendency to a special kind of abbreviation : the colo = colonie de vacances, the Catho is Catholic University, Frédo is Frederick, a prolo is a proletarian, a réco is a day of recollection, sympa is sympathetic, en perm = permission (i.e. leave), the Fédé is the Jocist federation. Then, too, there are vélo, apero, dactylo, typo and many others. I hope my readers will find the young prolos as sympa as I have during the weeks that I have been (imaginatively) living in their company.

Part III of this book may be called a documentary. I think it is important, but I am frankly puzzled about some of it. While reading it you must see in imagination a background of the France of at least the last hundred years : continually encroaching paganism, a Catholicism tied to all appearances to the old régime, a Catholicism losing bit by bit its property, its support from the State, its authority over education, its religious orders—perhaps its fervour ?

It is easy to exaggerate the defects and minimise the virtues of an age just behind us, partly because the defects were minimised and the virtues magnified at the time. There remained beautiful elements which prepared for the revival. But Père de Lubac takes (justly) a low view of the social qualities of a Catholic world which yet produced Frederick Ozanam. Léon Bloy took an even lower view, and his contemporaries did not like him. The Curé d'Ars and Sainte Thérèse seem rather by their blinding light to darken the surrounding picture: the Church at all times has produced great saints, but at some periods they show as typical, at others not. The saints and great men of nineteenth-century France in their reckless self-devotion are quite as untypical of the Catholics of their century as they are of the century itself.

I should be inclined—though dating is difficult—to say that the tide turned about the end of the first world war with the group of brilliant intellectual converts who followed close upon those two giants Léon Bloy and Péguy, and with that great man of action Cardinal Verdier, and that the change spread into another and wider world when the call to Catholic Action of Pius XI was taken up so ardently in France. But as Abbé Godin himself points out, all this has affected only the tiniest fraction of the population.

During and since the second world war we have the beginnings of another movement, potentially much wider and deeper. And my difficulty lies in determining how far this movement has penetrated. It is only too fatally easy when you are reading one kind of literature and meeting people all involved in a movement to see that movement as more widespread than it is. The optimists tell you that all France is on fire, the pessimists that only the tiniest flame has been lit. After all, they say, how many proletarian missions are there? Are there two score of priests involved? What do the lay teams amount to?

My own feeling is that the thing as a whole, while admittedly only a beginning, does amount to a good deal. The priest-workmen are more widely scattered than at first appears and the lay teams also. The Young Christians—workers, farmers, students, families—are a formidable army penetrating in many directions. The liturgical revival again is to be found in most unexpected places, the mass of missionary, liturgical and theological literature is not only printed, it is sold and therefore presumably read. If a flame, even a small flame, is lit in many parts of an area it soon becomes a conflagration. But this is a question that the next few years will answer. Meanwhile I have tried, especially in the third part of this book, to give some slight idea of France's answer to Abbé Godin's question.

CONTENTS

xi

CONTENTS

PART III

THE BREAD IS RISING

Part I

ABBÉ GODIN

I. PREPARATION

HENRI GODIN was born on Good Friday, April 13, 1906, at Audeux in the Doubs (Jura), a village of one hundred inhabitants, and baptised on Easter Tuesday. He often spoke of his peasant origin, but his father was actually a small, a *very* small, government official, drawing the princely salary of seventy francs a month. His mother did embroidery to augment the family income, but the children sometimes went hungry.

It was the height of the anticlerical régime—the time when monks and nuns were being driven into exile and churches turned into national monuments. Godin père was in the ambiguous position of being both a pious Catholic and a servant of the state. He went with his family to Mass and also to Vespers. If he could not get to church he would recite Vespers in Latin with the children. Yet ordered, on the separation of Church and State, to remove the crucifix from the law courts, he " suffered cruelly ", but he obeyed.

The children were sent to the village school, where Henri got high marks for composition but none for spelling. (Later at the seminary he struggled with this defect—copying whole pages from his dictionary, learning lists of words—but never with complete success.) At school he crossed swords with his master, refusing to be seated next to a girl and winning his point; and with one of the women teachers, writing an essay attacking a dance at which he knew she had been present during the war. " People who amuse themselves while others are dying." " If the soldiers could see this it would make them very unhappy." She had the sense to give him a good mark and only commented unfavourably on his spelling!

Henri liked to carry about in his pocket large pieces of broken bottles, to look at the scenery through bright green or blue glass.

3

His mother forbade this, but it still went on. (Poor woman, how many holes did she have to mend in his trousers?) He liked, too, to throw stones into a pool that reflected the night skies—" to make the stars jump ".

Home life did not last long : at twelve Henri was off to the Petit Séminaire. Difficult to say how young he was when he first thought of the priesthood. He had made his first communion at six and prayed on that day and at every subsequent communion, through Our Lady, that he might be a good priest, that, as he later phrased it, " if I were not to become a good and holy priest but a lukewarm and indifferent one I should be kept from becoming one at all ".

At the Petit Séminaire he was called " the saint " or " the monk "—the latter partly because of a cloak he wore with a large hood, partly because his silence and recollection led the boys to think he would enter a religious order. His health was miserable and he was a constant prey to headaches. For six months he was taken out of school and sent—a curious remedy —to be a chemist's assistant. It was heavy work and sometimes dangerous : washing out bottles, pouring disinfectants into them, lifting and carrying, dealing with acids and chemicals of all sorts. He was, too, working for a harsh master. But he felt later that these six months had been invaluable for a first-hand experience of a worker's life.

What impression did he produce on others ? That he was not very good at the job. That his overalls were in an awful mess. That he welcomed customers with quiet courtesy. That he refused cakes, especially on Fridays and in Lent.

Two visits to Lourdes brought no cure for the headaches but an answer to the prayer for strength to go on, and Henri Godin was able, though with constant difficulty, to get through his course at the Grand Séminaire. He was obviously a lad of a very high degree of intelligence, but he makes the interesting confession : " Philosophy seems to me the most stupid thing imaginable, yet I do want to care for it." Canon Glorieux in his biography casts an interesting light on this avowal. Godin, he

says, had " an instinctive need which was absolutely fundamental in his intellectual make-up, of translating the truths he
had discovered into the terms of life ". He was, thinks his
biographer, a man who, " letting himself go in the speculative
field, might have met with doubts and known temptations against
the faith ". From this he was saved by his energy in " realising
the living synthesis " of a Christianity not abstract, but one
in which truth was incarnated in " the details of the daily life
of a son of God. No gap between contemplation and action,
between speculation and practice."

His retreat resolutions are a mixture of ardent spirituality
and attention to external details: later he resolved to take for
his particular examination of conscience one supernatural and
one natural defect, e.g. his bad spelling. At the seminary he
resolved not to kid people more than he could help and planned
each day as to studies, prayers, spiritual reading, intentions,
meals, recreation. One note reads: " *Monday* tidy my clothes,
Tuesday shave, *Wednesday* walking shoes, *Thursday* turn my
mattress ", Friday is omitted, " *Saturday* straight to the
chapel, *Sunday* re-read my plan of meditation."

But above all Henri was preoccupied by the thought of what
it meant to be a good priest, a priest of the first quality, and
what means he should use to become one.

From the very first, even before his special apostolate had
become clear to him, he had seen Holy Orders as a social
sacrament—he had envisaged his priesthood not as something for
himself, but for others. To this his work at the seminary must
tend. He made endless notes—of retreats, of lectures, of his own
thoughts. " A doctor puts out a plate at his door, ' M.D.' He is
a murderer if he is incapable of curing the sick. A priest goes
into the confessional: in doing so he is undertaking to give
correct guidance, to indicate how sin is to be avoided and the
obligatory works of justice fulfilled. If he makes a mistake through
his negligence he is obliged to repair the harm he has done.

" So, too, in the pulpit. Something said wrong may throw
the faithful off the track. A feeble argument may prevent the

return of an unbeliever—'If that's all they've got to say for themselves'."

On the duty of charity and restraint in speech he confesses a special difficulty arising from his " need to talk", and makes firm resolutions. Interested in many things, he limited strictly the field of amusement, making especially repeated resolutions against listening to the radio for more than one hour daily. He had a passion for the radio. He notes that during one vacation he had practically never turned it off at all!

" Negative rules: not to be a priest-photographer, or a priest-radiographer, or a priest-beekeeper, or a priest-speculator. Simply to be a priest. You don't become a priest for your family, or for your mother, or your sister, but only for God. The priest's employment is not gardening or entertaining his fellow-priests agreeably. It is saving souls."

And again:

" Isn't this the sort of life a parish priest lives in a small place (which is what is likely for me. I have no ambition certainly to have an important parish). Isn't he only busy on Sunday? Other days once his Mass is said he becomes an independent gentleman. Humanly speaking, his zeal won't be great. Isn't it the sort of life Epicurus dreamed of? A life for an intellectual man, a quiet unburdened life. . . .

" This is an exaggeration, but still I don't think it's a life that would do for me.

" I want to be at the service of souls from morning to night and sometimes from night to morning. I want in my priestly life to give myself at least as much hardship as if I were the father of a large family. So what? "

The " what " is discussed at immense length. Service of God and of God's people. How on the positive side will it best be carried out? Everything must be used in his church— everything modern, for instance, that is " good, beautiful, practical "—a loudspeaker, and amplifier, a peal of bells, electric light, plenty of air. Old churches often give the false impression that religion has grown old with the church: let there be statues that the people like : let there be plenty of vestments and ornaments changing with the seasons : the people, above all the young, love a church which they have beautified : as far as possible let them have their way. Clear out all the old lumber that makes the sacristies like second-hand shops : let them be bright and light with a carpet on the floor and pictures on the walls. Be firmly opposed to irreverence, but allow ways of intimacy with God. . . . And so on at some length, the whole ending with resolutions of present conduct as a preparation for the supreme task of making his people understand and worship. The resolutions, like almost everything he writes, are made to Our Lady. He has just received the minor order of Lector and from it he begins :

" Lector 1. I must learn to read well : fast enough and without hesitation in French and, above all, in Latin. With great care, and with your help, my Queen, I will manage this.

" 2. I must learn to play the harmonium . . . hymns and plain chant . . . I have been working at this for seven years and have got nowhere. . . . With your very special help, my Queen, and almost by a miracle, I may succeed.

" 3. I must take great pains with the services. Crowds of altar boys well turned out and trained. Good for the children, their parents, and everyone else.

" 4. I must get all the faithful to take part in the services. This is essential. To assist at Mass is not to be bored for half an hour while a priest makes meaningless gestures in front of a table. It is not even to say one's rosary. [A real participation] must be achieved.

" As to the means, I can work them out best on the spot. Recitation of the prayers in French, by one or by everybody, instruction of the faithful, above all congregational singing and ceremonial.

" Worship must be interesting, comprehensible, popular and alive. To achieve all this I must begin now to reflect a lot, to look into things, to ask many questions and, above all, to pray a great deal."

ONE DAY as Henri Godin returned home for the holidays after many months at the seminary one of his old friends remarked: " You've changed. You don't belong to our class any more."

It was a terrific shock. For, as he examined himself, he recognised that it was true. " I didn't think of them any longer as ' we ' but as ' they ' . . . I felt a sense of revolt. I wanted to remain one of the people, and I tried for some time to fight against the implacable law of the milieu.

" But actually I do pray to Our Lord for ' them '. I never think of saying, ' Lord Jesus, workman like ourselves ', but I pray, ' Lord Jesus, workman like them ' . . .

" This is how my mind, from the moment I began to think, set me the problem of the change of class. I wanted to acquire learning, I was obliged to, but why could I not do it without abandoning my own class which I loved like my own country ? And I was right to love it."

Godin set this down in a thesis which he wrote later: *Déclassement, religion et culture humaine. Essai de psychologie sociale,* which later still formed the basis of *France, Pays de Mission?* In the thesis he enlarges on this special element more than in the book. He relates a conversation he often had in different forms. Two young men come to see him.

" Yes, it's quite true really that the Church isn't for the workers. The Communists are right."

" Well, sit down and tell me what's wrong."

" We've come from the seminary. We've seen Jean who went there last year and our other old pals. Two just passed the Baccalauréat."

" Well, has the Church been murdering your pals ? "

"That's what it's like. They're not pals any more. They're not ours. They've been stolen from us. We tried to talk over our apostolate in the factories, like we used to, and in the working districts. They don't give a damn any more" (but the phrase was stronger).

Godin tried to answer, but another lad broke in, "They're bourgeois now. They don't care about the working classes. They're deserters. There ought to be a seminary for workmen where they'd stay workmen when they become priests. All priests are bourgeois."

Godin pointed out the priest's need for learning and remarked that he, like the rest, had had to get his Baccalauréat.

"You're not a bourgeois."

"Am I a workman? You see, a priest ought not to be either a bourgeois or a workman: he ought to have a way of thinking that is neither the rich man's nor the proletarian's. He should judge things like Christ who loves all men whatever their lot: if by his studies he becomes a bit bourgeois, he must try with all his strength not to remain so."

But within himself he felt an element of truth in what they said. And he was resolving to be a poor priest among the poor. He was beginning to plan the apostolate of the workers.

It seemed obvious at first sight that the best beginning would be to join a religious order. He thought of the Fils de la Charité, a new order destined especially for this purpose, and notes among his reasons:

"Because I desire the apostolate of the poor whom Jesus preferred, whose outlook I share more than that of the rich and who are too often left on one side.

"Because our town parishes are mainly bourgeois and the working element is absolutely deserted."

It was to be a complete renunciation. He wrote to his "poor little sister" to whose dreams this would come as the end. He was a little sorry for himself. He went to Lourdes and told Our Lady so:

"I had a mother, and because of you I haven't got her any

more. I had a sister and a brother. I had holidays, a radio, enjoyments, friends who were more than friends, who were brothers. I had freedom, I had the right to a few little human pleasures in life and now I haven't got them any more. I haven't got anything . . . and I've done it because of you. . . . I had a mother on earth. . . . Heavenly Mother, take her place. Instead of the thousand little pleasures of earth . . . give me souls. . . ."

The final period of Godin's preparation for the priesthood was spent studying at the Catholic University and helping in the suburban parish where the noviciate was situated. A born observer, he noted what he was gathering from his contacts. He makes a close analysis of the different social layers on the morning trains into Paris and the evening trains out: the manual workers, the bourgeois and the small clerks and shop-girls who do not quite belong to either class. Why, he asks, does that little shop-girl whose father and brother are labourers, whose home is in a proletarian area, try to play at being a fine lady? It is the influence of the atmosphere she works in. She has got out of her natural milieu, she is struggling with all her might to get into another milieu. . . . This problem was beginning to haunt him. Culture, religion, both driving people to a change of class.

For himself he had the formula; his old friends should say: " He belongs to us: you can see that. He has stayed one of us, but he isn't the same as us. He is a priest."

How was this to be worked out fully in his life? Before his ordination he requested of his superiors to set him to work among the workers. Ordained on Holy Saturday, April 15, 1933, he was sent to Saint Vincent de Paul at Clichy where he was in charge of the sacristy, the parish accounts, girls' club and summer camp, besides confessions, preaching and catechism. Here, too, he first met the Jeunesse Ouvrière Chrétienne and became one of their chaplains.

This parish experience, Godin felt, had at once enriched him and opened his eyes wider to the needs that were haunting him. He made abundant notes showing unusual power of selection and of getting inside the lives of others. There are descriptions, for instance, of a young man, then of a family, typical examples of the effects of unemployment during the depression.

For the unemployed boy the worst was the loneliness of it. " If only your old pals stuck to you, but they don't understand. To be one of the gang you must have cash. You go to the cinema, you go for a stroll, you drink a beer, you must pay your turn. They leave you when they always have to pay, they drop you. . . ." " If I only had twenty francs to get my cycle mended."

" No more family life," a young workwoman sobbed out her story. " I can't bear to live at home any more; I must go: no, I can't stand it. But where can I go? It doesn't matter where, I just can't stay. My brother John is the only one working, so he gives the orders and he's a beast. I can't stand it."

" What about your father?"

" He's unemployed. And he says that the one who eats what another man earns can't give orders. The one who brings in the money is the boss."

And again the girls who won't do " what the foreman wants " lose their jobs. Only his " little friends " are kept on. " You begin to wonder if it isn't better to sacrifice yourself so your parents don't starve. I'm the only one earning. My father's out of work." And the phrase recurs, " No matter how she earns it as long as we eat."

One of the best girls in the club told him, " We can't afford to get married because we're both out of work, and my fiancé says he can't wait any longer."

" I implored her to hold fast, but she interrupted me with a savage note in her voice that told me the damage was done. ' We still love one another. And then he's so unhappy. It's all he has. '

" A baby is on the way in a home of the unemployed. It is an enemy which will fight for your last pennies and want to

share your last mouthful. ' If only we could get rid of it.'
What can you say to them ? ' It only means one more little
misery: we're too many already. We can't do with any more.'

" I must stop. My journal would not be big enough to relate
one typical case of each kind of anguish suffered by those who
have lost their jobs. And it tears my heart out merely to relate
the facts."

He suffered with each one and each one felt it. But he was
beginning to suffer from something else: personal: unexpected:
doubts whether he could stay with the Order he had chosen.
He discusses the question at great length (usually talking to
Our Lady) in his spiritual notes.

The minor issue was the unadaptableness of parochial life
to the needs of the pagan masses, as hungry spiritually as they
were physically. " The Fils de la Charité," he noted, " like all
the clergy of Paris, remain static in their apostolate. Their
aim is to keep those they have—with a few conversions on the
side. In practice, this seems everybody's method."

And yet it was the founder of his Order, Père Anizan who,
years before *France, Pays de Mission?* came to be written,
came very close to the idea that Godin was to make his own.
" We must," he said, " return to the methods of the beginnings
of Christianity, get together the few families and scattered
faithful, unite them, train them, work at increasing their
numbers, in one word recreate *small Christian communities.*

" *This is the traditional method followed by missionaries in
pagan lands,* and it is the method that we should follow in
the parishes to be founded and in the parishes to be won back."

Great ideas take time to come to fruition, and, after all, the
time was not so very long since Père Anizan had begun his
work. He was a remarkable man of whom little is known
outside France. Born in 1863, son of a doctor, he lived adventurous days during the war of 1870, became first a secular
priest, then a Vincentian. He began every kind of work possible
at his own date, and many that were in advance of it: co-
operatives, popular libraries, plans for cheap cooking in poor

homes, etc. His lay assistants looked for work for the unemployed, whitewashed their houses, while the women continued the methods of Saint Vincent himself by visiting the sick, doing their housework, minding their children and mending their clothes.

Head of the French Vincentians, Père Anizan was caught in the flood of anti-modernism just before the war of 1914, delated to Rome by one of his own brethren and deposed together with his entire governing body for " social modernism ". When the war broke out he became a chaplain at Verdun, and amid the constant care for the sick and dying he thought out the possibilities of a new apostolate. Others besides himself had left the Order, but desired as keenly as he did a resumption of religious life. The French hierarchy and the new Pope, Benedict XV, united in pressing him to take over a parish at Clichy in the depth of the proletariat. Père Anizan was now ageing. He lived long enough to salute with enthusiasm the beginnings of Catholic Action and to give a definite shape t his own community where existence was to be one of entir love and devotion for the masses. " Let us embrace charity," he said to his sons, " as Saint Francis embraced poverty."

The tradition started by such a man must have left its mark on the young Godin. In later life he showed warm appreciation of the Congregation, and one of his closest friends, the Abbé Michonneau, remained a Fils de la Charité. But his actual departure was not quite the peaceful matter that his biographer implies. The superior wanted to keep him: Godin was determined to leave, and the clash of wills as related to me by an intimate friend of Godin's appears to have been no slight matter. The little abbé could be firm to rigidity when clear that he was on the right lines.

The major issue for him was as ever the question of the degree of poverty that he personally felt obliged to practise.

Poverty is a relative matter: we have all heard of the poor American capitalist who in the depression got down to his last million ! The small bourgeois or the farmer is rich in the eyes of the clerk or peasant. But the peasant with a goat and a garden may seem wealthy to the proletarian. Henri Godin had been brought up as a poor boy in a poor village: now he was encountering that very different thing, destitution.

Here are a few of his notes:

" You do not want me," he tells Our Lady, " to have more luxury than I would have had if I had stayed in the world; to have what would make my brother say, ' You've struck lucky; you've had much better luck than me.'

" I was born of the people, and I should be betraying the people; I would be giving up something I could keep, something that characterises them: a very simple way of living."

Life in the Order was certainly not objectively luxurious: Godin equates it to certain homes among the workers where there are no children. But even this, he feels, appears to offer an excuse " for the great crime of those who won't have children".

" I know that what is luxury for me is an absolute matter of course for men with a different upbringing.

" But I judge with my lower-class outlook. And that is the class we are going to be judged by. . . .

" I do not blame: indeed, I understand. Education, atmosphere, tradition, necessities of which I know nothing, may tie the Fils de la Charité to a kind of life I don't like. I admire everything else about them. I don't blame this, but I see things differently."

A litany to Our Lady written earlier, to which he had added fresh invocations as time went on, throws further light on these notes:

" From becoming a bourgeois priest, deliver me, Mary.
From forgetting that I am poor, that I have always been poor;
From forgetting those who suffer;
From spiritual selfishness;
From the ecclesiastical spirit;

14

From having no sickness to suffer from, no griefs, no disappointments;
From seeing all the difficulties when undertaking any work;
From getting used to my Mass, to Jesus my God in the host;
From getting stale in my ideals as priest;
From professionalism;
From lack of confidence in you, deliver me, Mary;
From forgetting to think, to speak of you;
Above all—above all from not growing in your love;
Deliver me from my laziness, my incapacity (anyhow a little);
Mother, deliver me from man;
From pleasure;
From forgetting my working, suffering brothers;
From loving my family less;
From not remaining a poor little religious;
From despising the details of your service;
From scandalising anyone, however slightly."

To be delivered from man meant no doubt from human respect. And this was part of the struggle. Many would judge him unstable, changing for the sake of change. He had given up diocesan for religious life: now he was giving that up. But in October 1934 he was accepted by the Abbé Guérin for the national organisation of the J.O.C., thus becoming wholly devoted to the apostolate of the workers.

THE Young Christian Workers are an answer to Pius XI's call to Catholic Action for the laity. They are associated with the Church's missionary activity: they bear a share of the responsibility for it. Their organisation is built upon the Pope's formula: that every man must evangelise his own milieu: the doctor his fellow-doctors; the artist his fellow-artists; the workman his fellow-workmen. In France the J.O.C. and the J.O.C.F. are the masculine and feminine branches of the Jeunesse Ouvrière Chrétienne which has turned into the names Joc and Jocist. The J.A.C. is the Jeunesse Agricole, the J.E.C. the Jeunesse Etudiante, the J.I.C. the Jeunesse Indépendante.

The idea of Catholic youth organisations was not a new one. In the eighties of the last century Count Albert de Mun had launched the Association Catholique de la Jeunesse Française which in Belgium became the A.C.J.B. And it was from Belgium that the genius of Canon Cardijn sent back to France in 1927 the new movements which are proving so much more powerful and effective than their forerunners. One great difference between the two kinds of movement is paralleled by that between the Boys' Brigade with its regimental style, drill, marching, banners, etc., and the Boy Scouts with their personal development, less orderly, less impressive in a march or display, but with an internal vitality that is far greater. Thus, too, the older Catholic movements drilled the young, put on splendid displays, gathered them in halls and lectured to them, yet failed on the whole to generate a self-moving internal life.

The essence of the J.O.C. as of the other specialised movements is that it seeks to develop in the young real personal thinking from which action shall spring. They are not to be told what to do: they are to discover it. Their chosen formula is: see: judge: act. At a jocist meeting subjects will be brought forward for discussion, such as the conditions of work in the factory, the family or personal difficulties of a member of the group or of his friends, the way to bring back a lapsed comrade. All these problems are examined in the framework of daily life and of the Gospels. Practical resolutions are taken and tasks confided to various members—and one job at the next meeting will be to examine whether these assignments have been carried out.

Clearly for such a programme a small group is indicated: it is called a section. A number of sections is gathered into a local federation, local into regional and regional into national federations. Here again we see an interesting contrast with movements of the older type which began at the centre and gathered in members into one huge society with local branches. These specialised movements start small—with cells or sections growing outwards always organically, often slowly. The numbers have actually become enormously impressive, but numbers are not the first aim.

The term " specialised " can be understood best in relation to the way in which these groups function and grow. A mass movement gathered to listen, demonstrate and applaud could be composed of very heterogeneous elements. And, too, the old time organisations were concerned only with the leisure hours of those who joined them. These new societies have taken for their motto " to put the whole of Christianity into the whole of life ". And this life is *their* life: lived among certain people, occupied with certain employments. The people are to be won to Christ, the employments sanctified through Christ. A factory worker's environment is not the same as a student's, and both are widely removed from the world of the farmer. The technique of the different groups is strikingly similar. All use the Enquiry method. All treat as essential a living participation in the Liturgy, Gospel discussion, personal effort on society and on one's own life. But there must also be wide differences if each movement is to win its own world. And the passage of time (twenty-two years) has brought with it certain developments. The Jocist movement is for working youths and young men from their entry into work. Pre-Jocist groups have been started to prepare younger boys for their life as workers. The leaders are known as militants. They have special meetings of their own and are prepared more completely than the rank and file to give everything: in the words of Canon Cardijn, " to bring all the young workers and all the world of labour to a realisation of its divine origin and destiny."

The nature of the movement is thus a threefold one: to educate the young worker, to serve the young worker, to represent the young worker.

As the first generation of Jocists married the L.O.C. was formed (Ligue Ouvrière Chrétienne) which later turned into the Mouvement Populaire des Familles. The L.O.C. was at first modelled too closely on the youth organisations to be entirely suitable for adults, whose present organisations are strong and are growing stronger.

Naturally enough Abbé Guérin thought that a little more study of the whole business would make a good foundation for a life's work and for this purpose he sent Godin to Lille to study at the Catholic University.

This period he felt later to have been of tremendous import-ance in his life, but he also wrote of it, " Lille, terre d'exil." Canon Glorieux feels that the conventionality of a suburban town like Lille was far less fitted to Godin's temperament than Paris. But also he was trying to do the impossible. He was sick of books and expressed it characteristically in the remark that he didn't believe in ideas: but he had to study and to write. He was impassioned by his apostolate and was trying to carry out the two things simultaneously. A note, perhaps faintly malicious, in the news sheet linking past and present students, ran:

" Take notice . . . that it sometimes happens that Abbé Godin . . . takes a few lectures on the wing in between two meetings of unemployed. Moreover, as he has taken over $n+1$ Jocist sections scattered in the four corners of the world of Lille and even beyond, the Catho [Catholic University] may be said to be approximately the centre from which his influence radiates. So there you are!"

It is now that we begin to have a picture of Godin painted by the many who came to know him at Lille.

His devoted disciples in the J.O.C. often insist on the proof he furnished that one must not judge by appearances. His cassock was too short, his collar was always sticking out at one end, his hat was battered. " He was," says one, " a walking chaos." Those who served his Mass noted his innumerable mistakes, such as leaving out the Orate Fratres (an odd mistake for one who so identified himself with his congregation). He had a " sing-song voice " and a provincial accent. He would carry his money in a knotted handkerchief, would come to the meetings by bus or tram, cycle or car, through drenching rain or bitter cold, getting home perhaps in the small hours. " When he came in a car he didn't lack adventure. One night it had to be repaired at the club where a young mechanic happened to be present. For an hour the mechanic and his group of friends were secretly enjoying themselves at the expense of the poor priest with his pitiable appearance and downcast eyes. . . . Did he notice? One could never guess."

Probably he did, for he was an acute observer, of himself and of others. Among his spiritual notes are repeated resolutions against timidity, against too much imagination and " émotivité " and repeated expressions of his fear of not being enough of a man. To others he gave an impression of boldness, or even over-boldness. He was not so by nature: it was only by prayer and resolution that he forced himself to it.

On the question of his mechanical skill the most opposite opinions are expressed by those who knew Godin later on in Paris. Abbé Michonneau calls him " an exceedingly practical man—a first-class handyman. By vocation an electrician, he had an extraordinary power of picking up the skills of any other trade. How he transformed his own car! (Elsewhere spoken of frequently as ' the legendary little Simca. ') To what treatment had the poor thing to submit during his three years' ownership! But whether it was a matter of discussing their trade with his lads or turning his hand to the job: a repair to his bureau or anything that needed fixing, the abbé threw himself into it . . . on his desk, hammer and nails, etc., lay side by side with documents, letters and pens."

And some of his young disciples were in admiration of the alliance between knowledge and practical activity in their abbé. He could tell them all about " the architecture of a church, the evolution of medicine, the various types of printing machines, the manufacture of toys. Besides, he didn't only know things theoretically. Who among those who knew him can fail to have found him, hands covered with grease, in the act of mending a machine, a boy's cycle or the baby-carriage of a young household. . . . I don't know if the little workman he had been was a skilful one, but we all know from having seen him that the priest was not afraid of dirtying his hands with hard manual labour. Didn't he offer to paint our home himself whenever he could find the time? "

But when I repeated this to M. Müller at the *Editions Ouvrières* and to a young workman in the shop, both broke into peals of laughter. " His motor-bike," said M. Müller, " was in a perpetual state of being repaired by him: it was never in use." " He once drove me in a car," said the young workman, " and we were on the pavement most of the way." And M. Müller concluded, " I suppose you could call him jack of all trades but master of none."

Such skills as he did develop were learned painfully in the school of experience. It was Godin's ambition to climb, as Chesterton might have put it, to the level of the common man. Manual labour was part of the road. Anyhow, here at Lille his efforts were under criticism.

When he offered to multigraph the leaflets of a Jocist section, " Good Lord! how badly he did them! And they were full of spelling mistakes. ' Chômeurs ' was written ' chaumeurs' and lots of other words were equally misused. We had to do them over again."

Arriving very late, through engine trouble, at a church where he was to preach, he stood at the altar rails to deliver the sermon, his hands covered with grease. But the congregation were in tears at his words: " That *is* a priest."

For this was the other side of him. At the meetings he spoke little, listening, bringing things to a point, awakening enthusiasm, and leading his boys to ardent and practical resolutions. " If he did not bring us method or organisation he breathed into us an ideal, he brought us a soul."

If lectures were only taken " on the wing ", study was deep and thought also. He was preparing the thesis to which his life and thoughts had been leading.

We have seen his feeling about the way in which the bourgeois mind had impressed itself on the only culture which priests and educated people had received, and hence on religion itself. After examining the nature of that culture he went on to consider the possibility of a workingman's culture, one which would enable him to educate himself without ceasing to be a worker. This culture must itself be partly formed in action and through work. " You must have seen unemployment very close to understand the importance of work as occupation, work as the frame for life, work as the means of development."

But if the bourgeois culture has impressed itself on religion it is even more certain that the workman is seeking a religion of his own. He desires not only a culture but a *mystique*, an idea to get excited about, to draw stimulation from. A *mystique* is for him more than money, more than bread. " The working class is disturbed, is suffering because its soul is lost. You can only raise it up by restoring that soul: and that soul even today is deeply religious. I see no popular culture without a basis of religion, whether it be Christianity, Socialism or Nationalism. I see no popular culture becoming world-wide, no hope of social and international peace, nothing vital, nothing true, nothing lasting without that religion which alone can give them the true scale of values—the religion of Christ."

There was much more than this in the thesis—which, however, was never published. On its first presentation the examiners asked if a bad joke was being played on them. Atrocious spelling, of course, bits of paper of all shapes and sizes, erasures, blots. After revision, however, the examiners gave him a " très bien "—but forbade him to publish. Canon Glorieux thinks that they felt that men's minds needed preparation for the startling facts he was revealing. That preparation was the work of all that was left of Godin's life.

In spite of the impression made on his fellow-students Henri Godin's own estimate of his time at Lille was that too much of it had been spent among books, too little in human contacts. He wanted no more study of the J.O.C. but work with it and with life. " If I am to be a federal chaplain, I should do it better, a thousand times better, as a curate, in spite of lack of time, than left free for it. I so lack practical experience, especially with the young." He regarded his spiritual life as essentially built into and part of his apostolate: hence, during this year, " my inner life has gone quite flat".

Side by side with his views of social doctrine he had been working out his spiritual theories :

The holiness of the priest consists in making himself the perfect instrument of his apostolate, which demands great virtue and a profound interior life. " The idea of working for oneself with the thought of giving to others out of one's abundance fills me with horror. . . . I would rather look straight at souls: hence my motto in this matter is simply: many souls."

It proved that work at headquarters would give him all the experience he could possibly need. From the moment of his arrival in August 1935 at the Secrétariat Général of the J.O.C. in Paris there were no more regrets, no looking back: the apostolate was full, rich and varied. Individual direction, guidance of sections of girls, young men and boys; sermons, retreats, one entire region to care for, helping with the general secretariate, with the Letters to Chaplains, fresh beginnings for adult Catholic action.

His life now becomes identified with the life of the Paris workers: Canon Glorieux quotes: " He needed the great anonymous crowd of the capital where conventionality had less hold than in the provinces." He made a special note to read the papers every day and to see his Jocist leaders constantly. He papered the walls of the Assembly Hall with posters of congresses and was enchanted by the symphony of colours in which red dominated. It raised the temperature of the meetings, we are told, which was probably what he had hoped. He was given a room on the seventh floor with a small study attached and there he remained until 1941 when a desire to get still closer to the workers brought him to the Rue Ganneron.

Always a great talker, he worked out his schemes with the priests at the centre. " He talked to me," says his superior, Abbé Guérin, " of his experiences, his projects, the books he was writing. His temperament and his theory demanded the reactions of someone in whom he had confidence. His schemes of work, his various projects: recollections, gatherings of chaplains, etc. I owe a great deal to those intimate talks."

They all ate together, anyhow at midday, which was as well for Godin as it meant at least one decent meal a day. In the evening he would be seen hurrying to a meeting munching a packet of biscuits by way of dinner. At mealtime at the centre he was amazingly gay, full of good stories, jokes, paradoxes, startling ideas.

Clearly he loved an argument. " He was characterised," his admirers confess, " by an instinctive opposition to conformity . . . His inclination was to turn upside down whatever was at all set. He valued anything new and original in what he undertook. It was with difficulty that he endured the demands of an orderly organisation, a detailed administration."

He scrupled very little to make changes in orders received or to substitute other activities for those laid down. He was considered by many too much of a free lance. And his admirers themselves were sometimes disconcerted when as they tried to abound in his sense, agreeing, adding confirmatory evidence, he would suddenly turn on them with, " I don't think that is quite the point."

Nor did this arise entirely from a spirit of contradiction. Godin felt strongly that there are several sides to everything and that they should all be examined before decisions are made. Still, " How he loved contradicting," says a priest-friend. But he would not make the decisions for his Jocists: that was to go outside what, in his judgment as well as by the theory of the movement, was the chaplain's province. It was also a profound instinct of leadership.

" He loved," says a Jocist leader, " to pose problems. Pose problems . . . and not offer solutions, for according to him that was the leaders' own job."

Yet clearly, as they talked and re-talked (*repenser* and *reparler* are favourite words of his), the solutions found by the leaders had been " in his head for a long while, but he wanted me to discover them for myself".

As a spiritual director he traces a similar programme, " to develop wills, not to replace them: education consists in making the educator superfluous."

And again, " To be the doctor of souls is an educative work. I am the mortal enemy of what is called direction. One should never force on others one's own lights, one's own methods."

The educational work was very thorough. " He taught me," one girl writes, " to plan my life so as to live the whole of it with God. Not a vague plan in the air but a precise forecast, noting on my agenda what I should have to do in the day, the time for getting up and going to bed, with a personal examination in the evening or next morning during my meditation. He never told me to use any pious book to make my meditation: life offers so many things to talk to God about and to go deeply into with Him: the difficulties of this or that militant, the discouragement one of the girls is feeling and the reasons for it, unemployment and all its results in somebody's life and many other things. Gone over again with Christ, all this began to take on a new aspect. One could do a very good job in this way."

Abbé Godin's friends in Paris, especially his young workers, supremely the girls, have far more (unconscious) art in presenting him to us than anyone at Lille.

" When I was president of my section," says one lad, " before the war I saw this abbé at federal councils. He seemed to be always in the moon, amusing himself during a meeting by taking his watch to bits or pricking his neighbours with a pin to make them jump." (Reaction against a series of dull speeches perhaps!) " To see him so white, so tired, I thought he must be going to leave his body and that he had not long to live.

" Then I was summoned to the Fédé. My first contact with him made me fancy he was a little mad. . . . And I was not far wrong, but I did not understand what a sacred madness it was that had seized him."

" He walked," says another, " with great strides in the streets of Vincennes, bare-headed, wearing huge hob-nailed boots; over his short soutane a sort of cloak of rough material fastened at the waist by a narrow leather belt. . . . He looked at nothing. When not praying he was thinking of his boys, his girls, his young couples, and asking himself if there was nothing more he could give them. What more could he have given us? He had given everything and having absolutely nothing left he went on day after day giving himself wholly to the winning of the workers."

" He was not a priest friendly to the people," another writes, " he was simply one of the people. We felt him so close to us in the whole of his life. He was so simple with us. He was like a big brother who often played the fool with us and squabbled with us, but for whom we had an affectionate respect. He was a real man. He needed to relax, and he did it with real enjoyment. What stories could be told of foolery set on foot by him! "

" He had an overful life," says Dr. Tremolière, " but he had a great power of relaxation. He would take one or another

team and go with one to the cinema, with another to camp. . . ."
And at the doctor's home " he often came to dinner. . . . I
can still hear his ' Good evening, Doctor ' with its curious
accent (franc-comtois) which made the phrase sing. . . . Often
he wanted us not to mention *at all* the problems that were
bothering him. He had come to relax and he played the fool
exactly like the peasants of the Jura mountains: that is to say,
he kidded you. The next day he sent a little card thanking for
the excellent holiday he had had with you and noting some
question brought to light by the foolery. . . . He adored fooling.
He told me how he once had to get into an overcrowded train
with a rather fat canon. Impossible to get in by the door so he
managed to get in through the window and wanted to get the
canon in in the same fashion. This story enchanted him."

The word " simple " recurs, sometimes used rather in the
sense of natural. Abbé Godin was at home with his workers.
" He lived in poverty, greater poverty than any of us." " He
didn't mind sleeping among us." He was detached from this
world's goods less, says one, from mortification " than from his
desire to keep in touch with the masses and his overwhelming
activity ".

Keeping in touch always seemed to him tremendously
important, not only for himself but for his militants. One girl
relates her own dismay because some of her section had had a
fist fight with some boys. The abbé said, " That's what the
masses are like: those are the people you can do the best work
with." Another time, after a study day, he said to the same girl,
" I'd like to see you and the rest of the committee more stylish,
with more make-up, like other girls. In fact, I want you to be
girls like the rest." It was so fatally easy to lose touch. One
leader relates how she went for a holiday to a Colonie de
Vacances (" to the Colo with our Fédé ") as a simple worker
and discovered from the talk of the other girls how hurt and
discouraged they often got by the way the leaders bossed them.
It was a revelation: " In one hour I understood what Père
Godin had been telling me for five years. From that moment

I had a limitless confidence in him. He helped me to grow young again and to plunge deeply into real action."

To be close to reality—"dans le vrai". Not to go out of their world, but as Christ had become incarnate in the world of man so to bring about a new incarnation of Him today. For we are all members of the Mystical Christ. " He lived the Gospel literally. That, no doubt, was why he could talk and write so well about Christ the Worker and His Mother and all the divine realities. His love of the humble must have been enormously pleasing to the heart of his Master."

They all felt he had an individual personal love for them. " A gift for loving you," one of them calls it. " He lived in the case you brought him, suffered or rejoiced and finally got at the heart of it. But in such a way that what he said after he had listened to you for ages gave you a feeling of setting you free, revealing you to yourself and setting your feet on a glorious road."

" He really loved those who came to him. He listened to them entirely self-forgetful. Then he would carry within himself this slice of another's life and reflect on it continually (nights were useful for this). Sometimes he was seized in this way by a case the day had brought him and he thought about it until two in the morning or later. Then after this painful effort of labour, he would bring forth words that revealed you to yourself and made you grow greater.

" This attentiveness to the actual human life that was around him, that is to say real charity, was his dominant characteristic."

The photographs of him are all, his intimates agree, rather unsatisfactory. I have chosen the one considered least unlike. But I think his mother must have tidied him up to have it taken! That in Canon Glorieux's book has an odd history: a snap-shot like the rest, it showed him originally with a big pipe in his mouth. Considered unedifying, the pipe was taken out, and the mouth suffered in the process.

To the student of Abbé Godin's life the title of his first book *Le Christ sur la Ligne Maginot* comes with a slight shock of surprise. In his biography the war is hardly adverted to. Probably this is largely because, although published after V-day, the book must have been in preparation during the occupation. But I think it is also because of the special bent of Abbé Godin's mind, the special direction his life had taken, which is indicated by a story he relates of the débâcle. Meeting a fellow priest,[1] a missionary from a far country, on the roads crowded with refugees fleeing before the German armies, Abbé Godin talked with him of the anguish that filled his heart. And this anguish was not that of the Frenchman over the plight of his country, but the anguish of the priest over the souls of the poor. It is refreshing to find a Frenchman whose first preoccupation is not France!

Of the time of the " phoney " war we learn only in a footnote to *Témoignages* that Godin was mobilised in 1939, was sent to Clermont-Ferrand as a private, and spent all the time he could beg or steal visiting Jocist sections in the neighbourhood. Talking with a man who had been with him I learnt that he made his mark in the army as so often elsewhere by his love of fooling. " If he was out on a holiday he was like a kid. I remember being in a boat with him when three of us couldn't swim and he kept trying to upset it."

Above their beds many of the men had pinned photos of naked women. Godin made no priestly protest, but pinned over his own the picture of an extraordinarily pretty, modest-looking girl. " This led to conversation," said his friend succinctly—and left me to imagine the conversation that it led to.

He made friends with anticlericals, Communists and atheists and one day took a bet with a rather inflated anticlerical who had been boasting of what he would say " to those curés "— " Would you dress up in a soutane and go and see one ? " said Godin as the talk went on. " Certainly," said the man. And Godin took a bet that he wouldn't. Presently he began to tell him how he would have to behave. The curé would certainly

[1] See below, p. 126.

offer him a meal: he must say the Benedicite: Godin would teach him: it wasn't too difficult. Bit by bit the man grew nervous until at last he called the bet off.

Even at that date, many country people were fleeing, remembering the last war. It was not the flood it became later, but refugees carrying their goods and their children were to be seen on the roads making their way towards friends or relatives in safer areas. Abbé Godin one day, dressed in uniform, was riding a motor cycle. A splendid car passed him in which was sitting a chauffeur, a well-dressed woman and a small colony of pet dogs. On the road a refugee with her children signalled vainly to the car which went by at top speed. Godin also speeded. He got ahead of the car and forced it to halt, removed the dogs, moved the owner into the front seat beside the chauffeur, managed to fit the refugee family and their bundles into the back seat, and then rode alongside until they were safely at their destination.

Afterwards he remarked, " It's certainly wonderful what can be done with a uniform."

Coming on to the occupation, we have again scant material for a picture: we must imagine shortages constantly increasing. We have seen our friends who lived through it in Paris, lost twenty or thirty pounds in weight and emerged looking like ghosts. For the very poorest it must have been an unimaginable nightmare. And Abbé Godin was of the poorest. The Simca had to be given up. Indeed it was the lack of all transportation other than cycles that made Abbé Guérin consent to Godin's transference to the Rue Ganneron. The cold was fierce in winter, little or no heating to be had, and we are told that he was naturally chilly.

The flat is three floors up and has a glorious view over Paris. Godin's little bedroom was also his study and reception room. Many of his friends were in the Maquis and he received domiciliary visits from the Gestapo. This did not fail to bring his rather puckish sense of humour into play, and he used to relate with chuckles how two Germans came one day, one quite good-natured, both intensely stupid, and asked him for a list of names. He answered that no doubt they could get them from the Cardinal-Archbishop of Paris. Out came a notebook, the Cardinal's address was solemnly taken down, Abbé Godin was thanked and left in peace! But he loved adventure, and would cross the demarcation line between zones dressed as a workman and without papers.

Aside from these stories we should hardly know the war existed but for its effects on the lives of the young Jocists who wrote to him from Germany or visited him " en perm ", or whose wives and fiancées received spiritual and sometimes material support from him while they were absent.

The one way to get a deported labourer home on leave was for him to be about to be married. So Godin would marry his Jocists—on paper: numbers of them would come home and return to Germany armed with a document that could be shown to the authorities. Godin was good at this matter of forged papers. If he himself wanted to visit a group in an area where a permit was needed he would stroll down to the office in question, slip into the men's room, emerging only after the office was locked up for the night. At dawn it was not too difficult to get hold of the necessary papers and before the hour for opening he would go into the men's room once more and only emerge when many other people, applying vainly for permits, made his exit sufficiently safe. He used to boast that while people with perfectly good papers got into trouble he always got by.

How Abbé Godin found time to write it is hard to say, but between March 1936 and January 1944 he actually published sixteen books of varying sizes. Some were little more than pamphlets. All except *France, Pays de Mission?* were intended for the workers and published by the *Editions Ouvrières*. " He wrote," says his biographer, " when he had ten minutes to spare: at night when he got home after a meeting, at mealtimes while he ate, absent-mindedly scratching away with his pen on a corner of the table, and again late into the night."

" He slept very little," says Doctor Tremolière, " going to bed at three or four and getting up at six. Latterly I almost succeeded in persuading him to go to bed not much later than twelve or one. Coffee helped him to keep awake and to go on working. When the black market became too difficult he drank Tonique Roche and the number of empty bottles of Tonique Roche measured the intensity of his work of the moment." (In theory a good afternoon siesta supplemented the short night's rest, but too often it remained theory.)

" Call Abbé Godin an author? " says his publisher, Marcel Müller. " Not on your life! But what was it that he had? Dynamism, the fire of an apostle, a passionate love of the working masses. And all these qualities were thrown into brief notes, written in haste, with utter indifference to what would be said of them, written between two interviews, broken into by telephone calls, or just after a meeting of militants, or in the evening until late into the night."

The publisher notes almost with surprise, " And yet the works of Abbé Godin have had and will continue to have a marvellous circulation, for they are crammed with vitality.

They have a freshness and sincerity and youthful drive that defy criticism and force an entry into men's hearts."

To a friend who suggested that he might polish and improve what he had written, Godin answered that plenty of people could be found later who would polish and improve. Essentially creative, he wanted only to get ahead with the vast work he had envisaged—a whole workers' library written by others as well as by himself and written in collaboration with others. For his workers' Missal he used several collaborators, one being set to translate the Epistles and Gospels, another the Mass prayers. He managed to get his idea over even to the printers who were setting the Missal—they worked with such fervour that he said one day after visiting the presses, " This is really the Redemption in action."

One of his collaborators, Doctor Tremolière, produced under the pen-name Doctor Jouvenroux a remarkable book, *A la Découverte d'Amour* : there was a *Collection Mariage*, a *Collection Culture Nouvelle*, a *Collection Jeunesse*, a *Collection Noël*. And the J.O.C. themselves put out a series entitled *A la Découverte*.

Le Levain dans la Pâte is a characteristic and interesting specimen of Godin's work. Not for one moment does he lower his ideas or his ideals to adapt them to the masses. It is the highest of spiritualities, that of the Gospels, deeply implanted in the human life of today. The only concession made for those who read little except the newspapers is in the arrangement—which is rather teasing to an accustomed reader. There are an enormous number of different types used; small and large, light and very heavy. This with the headlines and the inset illustrations makes it very like reading a daily paper— but one in which the Good News of the Gospel has become news once more. How Chesterton would have loved it!

The matter, like the letterpress, is immensely various. There are quotations from Péguy and Claudel, from Marie Noël and Francis Jammes, from Verlaine and Fagus. There is a brilliant page in the style of Péguy:

God talks to man about how He made the world and how He intended it to work. Made in His image, man has a mind to think with, a heart to love with.

> " ' Moi,' dit Dieu, ' je n'agis que pour amour, et eux-mêmes ne peut rien faire de grand sans amour.' "[1]

When a man gives you a machine to look after, he gives you the directions you are to follow. Otherwise there will be accidents. God's directions for His marvellous machine, the Universe, are the Ten Commandments; which are all summed up in one: to love one another, to be united. His Son came to teach men love, and men crucified Him. His Church has tried. The Pope has tried. And yet, and yet, they live by the motto " Each man for himself."

> " Résultant: Luttes—Crise—Guerre—Souffrances—Morts. ' C'est décourageant,' dit Dieu, ' Je ne sais plus que faire avec eux.' "[2]

And now these men whom He still loves as His children begin to accuse Him of what their own motto has produced, they even say: if there were a good God there wouldn't be so much suffering.

> " 'C'est tout de même fort, ça,' dit Dieu, 'c'est un peu trop fort!' "[3]

What do they want God to do, punish by thunder and lightning and kill a lot more people?

> " 'Ah ça non,' dit Dieu, 'ce n'est plus mes méthodes, ce n'est pas éducatifs.' "[4]

---

[1] " Myself," says God, " I do nothing save for love, and men can't accomplish much without love either."

[2] Result? Conflict—Crisis—War—Suffering—Dead men.
" It's discouraging," says God, " I simply don't know what to do with them next."

[3] " And really that's tough," says God, " it's a bit too tough."

[4] " Not possibly," says God, " those aren't my methods, they're not educative."

To do that would be to destroy their liberty and make them like animals.

" J'ai fait mes enfants libres, c'est en cela qu'ils me ressemblent.
Leur retirer leur liberté, ce serait supprimer les hommes de la terre." [1]

God has at least made it possible that men may draw some profit for the next life out of the mess they insist on making of this. Yet He wants them happy in this life too; but

". . . il faut qu'ils comprennent bien une chose:
Qu'ils n'ont pas à m'accuser de leurs fautes,
(Ça, c'est facile . . . Comme ça, les responsables disparaissent),
Mais qu'ils ont a reparer leurs erreurs et leurs crimes.
Et, pour cela, dit Dieu, je suis prêt à les aider." [2]

In this squat little volume are poems, pictures, stories, sketches. The young workers were to have song and joy and love brought back to them. They need not be deprived of knowing the great writers of their country, only the passages must be chosen for them that they could read and understand.

Many of the books are written in a way that might easily become artificial but is here profoundly real. Godin would gather a group of young men or women and discuss with them the problems of life, getting from each a genuine contribution. "When," says Doctor Tremolière, "he asked Odile or Andrée for her experiences it was not in order to place them in a pre-determined category that fitted the idea already in his mind.

---

[1] I have made my children free, it's by that that they resemble me.
To take away their liberty, would be to abolish *men* from the earth.
[2] . . . one thing they must grasp:
That they haven't me to blame for their faults.
(That's the easy way. . . . Like that, there'd be no responsible beings left),
But that they have to repair their errors and their crimes.
And for that, says God, I am ready to aid them.

It was with those big child-like eyes of his, astonished at everything, attracted by everything alive."

In *Le Christ sur la Ligne Maginot* we have a group of soldiers,
in *Jeunesse qui reconstruit* boys and girls in a factory, in *Jeunesse
qui s'épanouit* problems of love and marriage seen through the
eyes of young lovers, husbands and wives. Drawn thus from
real and not fictitious experience these books are intensely
alive, the characters are people. We suffer when a boy dies on
the Maginot Line, we rejoice when a young couple are married,
we smell the stew served in the canteen of the factory, and
we are aware of the occasional tension between old and young
workers, of the quarrels and reconciliations of lovers. The
thought is developed through and in their life.

Anxious that they should read and love Scripture he makes
use of these groups to initiate discussions that shall bring the
Gospels into close contact with daily life. It is open to doubt
whether it is entirely wise to have done this by using a para-
phrase rather than the text itself. Considering the high level of
thought to which he was lifting them it seems incredible that
they could not have followed the Gospel words: the best of
paraphrases involves a diminution and this is not always the
best. The Apostles were not merely " twelve militants ", nor
is Our Lord's way of talking to them well conveyed by such a
sentence as, " Dîtes, les gars, vous n'auriez pas quelques
poissons à me donner à manger? "

With Godin's own work it is, however, chiefly a question
of taste: there is substantial fidelity to the original. But the
method is a risky one, and with some of his imitators the
paraphrases become markedly tendencious as they move further
from the text of Scripture into the glow of the paraphraser's
imagination. Not for nothing does the Church guard jealously
the integrity of the text.

Even the discussions themselves may go too far against the
old method of teaching the young and in favour of the new
method of letting them find out for themselves.

When Newman had first made his way out of his early

Calvinism he noted that ordinary men were capable of being taught far more of the truths revealed in Scripture than they could themselves discover. They could assimilate, make their own, *live by* truths they could not find for themselves. After all, we do believe in a teaching Church. And one cannot quite see why *in a book* some few words could not have been added, taking the reader a little further forward than the young group could go alone. This applies both to truths of faith and facts of history. When, to take one small instance, they compare the Pharisee to a rich bourgeois kneeling in the front bench and the publican to a poor proletarian at the back, it might have been worth telling the other young who would come to read the book what Pharisees and publicans really were—that the publican was probably richer than the Pharisee and certainly just as bourgeois!

This is all the odder in Godin considering that he was a born teacher. The books, the days of study, and supremely the retreats and recollections, were all methods of education. And when one meets any of his young disciples, one is immensely struck by the high degree of culture they have reached, the power with which they can seize and analyse their problems, the depth and height of their outlook. There was something creative in his education. Speaking of a distinguished theologian, he said, " These people don't *think*—our theologians *don't think*." And he desired by *thinking*, in relation alike to theology and to his proletarians, to bring about a fresh uprising of Catholic thought in their midst. " He gave," says Doctor Tremolière, " a very wide meaning to the word *popularisation*. It meant to adopt the way of thinking and of feeling that belongs to a certain world in order to express for that world truths that have been the preserve of the initiated. In this popularisation he saw one aspect of the Incarnation. To popularise successfully one must really live the life of those one is speaking to—one must love them and live *their* life."

It is interesting to learn that Godin found Péguy the writer most appreciated by his young proletarians. And it is again in the fashion of Péguy that he himself expressed for them his own most characteristic thoughts on love and marriage, on Our Lady and the ideal of womanhood.

God begins by saying that there are people who don't like the way He has made the world and who would like to get all the women together in the northern hemisphere and the men in the southern with a barrier at the equator: a wall ten yards high with broken bottles at the top. But God doesn't make barriers; He knows, for He made men, that they can't be happy with a barrier:

" Ils ont besoin de femmes pour aimer, pour se grandir et
        être heureux.
    ' Je n'aime pas beaucoup les vieux garçons,' dit Dieu." [1]

Woman is the best gift God has given to man.

" 'Et je ne pouvais pas lui faire un plus grand:
    Et quand j'ai envoyé mon Fils sur la terre, Il n'a pas été
        difficile.
    Ah! ça non, IL N'A PAS ÉTÉ DIFFICILE, ni pour la nourri-
        ture, ni pour le logement, ni pour la condition,
    Ni pour rien sauf pour sa mère. Alors, là, Il a été
        DIFFICILE . . .
    Il a voulu un CHEF-D'ŒUVRE DE MÈRE qui dépasse même
        mes anges, qui sont déja de bien grands chefs-d'œuvre.
    Ah! pour cela, il a été DIFFICILE. Pour la femme qui
        devrait lui donner le jour, et éveiller son âme, et former
        son cœur.
    Et les hommes sont pareils. Choisir une femme, c'est
        toujours le grand affaire de leur vie.
    Ça ne m' étonne pas,' dit Dieu." [2]

---

[1] They need women if they are to love, to grow and to be happy.
" I'm not very fond of old bachelors," says God.
[2] "A greater gift I could not give him.
And when I sent my Son on earth, he was not hard to please.

Looking over my shoulder as I read a friend remarked,
" The Young Christian Workers must have very good eye-
sight." And I realised that the infinitesimal print of these
books had given me a bad headache. I explained to the publishers my difficulty in reading them and they held up their
hands in despair. Abbé Godin, they explained, was always
determined to put on every page one and a half times what
that page would hold. He hated to see any white space at all,
said M. Müller gloomily. He knew nothing of layout. And one
would call on him to finalise the plans for a book only to find
oneself the fourth or fifth person in his tiny room. He would
be carrying on five conversations simultaneously amid constant
telephone rings. The MSS. had to be assembled: here were
some pages in the centre drawer of his desk, more in the right-
hand top, the left-hand bottom, others scattered about the
room. One was lucky if one could carry it away in anything
near a completed condition.

As a publisher myself I could not but sympathise. The
layout of the books is far inferior to other work of the same
house. Yet the abbé had a sense of beauty that resulted
in much better illustrations than those, for instance, in
other people's books illustrated by the same artist. He knew
what was good and would unhesitatingly reject what was
bad.

Most of his books are richly illustrated, with things old and
new. He used to love to collect in a drawer beautiful photographs, reproductions of great pictures, anything that might
serve later. It reposed him to look at these. He would talk

No, he was not hard to please—either about food, or lodging, or state in
life, or about anything, except his Mother. But about her he was
exacting.
He wanted his mother to be a masterpiece, surpassing even my angels,
who are already very great masterpieces.
Yes, for her he was exacting—for the woman who was to bring him into
the world and awaken his soul and form his heart.
And men are like him. Choosing a woman is always the great affair of
their life.
Which doesn't surprise me," says God.

them over with his visitors. He wanted people to think about beauty and to pray about it.

The wife of a prisoner of war tells the story of her collaboration with him when she was illustrating *Jeunesse qui Chante*. She had received a note from *Editions Ouvrières* asking her to call at the Rue Ganneron. She climbed the many stairs, got her breath at the top, heard shouts of laughter, and went in to find in a tiny kitchen a boy and a girl holding hands and a priest sitting at a littered table.

" It was Monsieur l'Abbé Godin: his keen, lively, piercing eyes gazed at us over the top of his spectacles, his calm simple face wore a pleasant smile, he had a beard of three days' growth and his fingers were covered with black and purple ink.

" In a singing voice with a fine racy accent he said, ' Good morning, Madame Gaillard. Here are Riton and Paulette, engaged to be married. Do you like flowers? I need some beautiful drawings with little birds and sunshine. You see it is for *Jeunesse qui Chante*.'

" An odd way of doing business! To act normally myself, I tried to talk about technique, procedure, methods of work. I soon saw that my new employer was not the least interested in that sort of thing. By now I began to feel confused and uncertain. But the work, once begun, was passionately interesting because at the same time I was living the joy of *Jeunesse qui Chante*, and beginning to understand the unfathomable riches of Abbé Godin's soul.

" Poor *Editions Ouvrières*—how they must have torn their hair! For two years I was working for Père Godin amid confusion and mirth. Short notes sent by special delivery signed with the usual H.G., filled with appalling mistakes, illegible; changes of format, things taken out, things put in, discovery of new subjects for drawings not forecast in the estimates of the *Editions Ouvrières*.

" I had to finish in two nights for my boss, Père Godin, twelve drawings which fifteen days later I found lying in his drawer. But what did that matter? He might throw in some spelling mistakes, forget a detail, lose a drawing, while his mind, the mind of a saint and a genius, was working out plan after plan of books that might make an army of devils turn to God— and all this in the middle of all his other activities.

" Good heavens, what sort of man was he? He was a saint. Not a man like other men; a poor man liberated from all earthly riches but possessing a limitless treasure of the spirit."

By THIS time Godin had stripped himself more completely than ever. Even at the Fédé he had begun to be afraid he was too comfortable. " Can I be a real Christian while leading this bourgeois life when Our Lord has made me understand so clearly that it displeases Him?

" To do the opposite means to become abnormal. The poor have demands on me, but ecclesiastical conventions have greater demands and I am being carried away by them.

" My God, help me to see straight."

Godin being Godin, we are not surprised that the next stage had been the little flat in the Rue Ganneron, where, says Madame Gaillard, he would probably not even have eaten if his young friends hadn't put potatoes in his bin surreptitiously. Others tell of how they came round and cooked him a meal and then helped him to eat it in his minute kitchen, where you couldn't move away from the heat and your legs felt scorched.

It was all part of the self-forgetfulness spoken of by so many. He literally forgot to eat. Yet he could appreciate a feast at the house of a friend, and, above all, could take pleasure and pride in his mother's good cooking when he took a friend home to have dinner in the family circle.

Home meant an enormous amount to Henri Godin. Clearly he had dreamed of a presbytery with his mother and sister at hand and had renounced it for his workers' apostolate. But still, says Abbé Michonneau, he drew his whole family into his orbit; his sister especially helped with his work, multigraphing his outlines for recollections, copying his manuscripts (perhaps correcting the spelling?). After his sister's premature death— *the* great grief of his life—the brother took over these tasks.

" You ought to see him among his own people. I have seen him hanging round the neck of his old mother, swinging her round, almost dancing her like a baby. The poor woman struggling to get free could not stop herself from bursts of laughter at the ' little man's ' antics."

The sacrifice of the priest in giving up family life had been made in its fullness by Henri Godin. " I was sad at first when I thought about that ' always '," he told Our Lady on the eve of his subdiaconate, " because you have given me a loving heart and when I see a little boy or girl I feel a bit envious. Let me admit it, I no longer feel like an older brother, but like one who might have been the father they are loving and coaxing."

At twenty he would not have felt it so much: now he realised better the need of loving and being loved. " If I love you I shall be happy, if I do not love you I shall be unhappy and sinful. Unhappy because I shall have to be satisfied with stolen crumbs when I might have sat at table, sinful because I have promised all my love to you. Even the stolen crumbs of what would have been good and healthy will be bad. So there is nothing left for me but to love you passionately."

And then he found that with God's love came a fulfilment of his own human longings, not only in the love of the children of his adoption, but more especially in the place he held in their homes. Again and again they tell us of his joy in their engagements, in their marriages. Nothing, they say, made him so happy as when Riton brought Paulette to make him the first sharer in their joy, unless it was to marry them, to visit them later, to baptise and bless their babies, to help them in their difficulties.

These marriages usually turned out well—thanks in part to Godin's unusual insight. He would introduce to one another two Jocists likely to be " sympa ", he would warn a boy keeping company with a girl who would not suit him. Sometimes real tragedies were averted—a Jocist advised by Godin to give up his first fancy found she had been going with another man and was about to have a baby. When he was in doubt about the suitability of a couple to each other, he would say, " I'll talk it over with God."

It was in the Rue Ganneron that Abbé Godin's greatest apostolate began: that of the Jeunes Foyers, or young married couples. As with everything else in his life, theory was never separated from experience. In the little flat besides Godin's study-bedroom and the kitchen is a pleasant, larger room which any man but he would have kept for himself. But this room, Abbé Hollande told me, was latterly usually occupied by a young houschold. Earlier it was a place where anyone might sleep. Dédé and Madeleine, who were its last tenants, relate how Abbé Godin had got Dédé back from Germany by managing to procure forged papers for him, how it was not safe for him to go home because the Gestapo was watching the house. " So we lived in the Rue Ganneron. The baby was on the way. Madeleine did the cooking and the abbé used to tease her, saying, ' This little girl doesn't know how '."

How practical was his touch on their lives may be seen by a little letter to Doctor Tremolière:

" DEAR DOCTOR,

" Madeleine's ultra nervous state is really a serious handicap [spelt endicape] for the family. The priest will engage himself seriously in handling it and perhaps the doctor could help, too. . . .

" Très fraternellement,

" H. G."

" The priest should go to the home," Godin wrote. " The atmosphere of the home is almost indispensable to the solution of the problems of the home. Only there is to be found that peace, that warm affection which help a real unveiling of the soul.

" The priest who has given up a home to help others has the graces of his state to hear everything in holiness and purity. If openness of heart is full between husband and wife it will be easy for them to talk to the priest for they will talk like they do to one another."

He became then the director, not of husband or of wife, but of homes, helping them both spiritually and materially. A baby was on the way, he said Mass for the mother; a husband was taken prisoner, he gave them both " doses of courage ", taught them how to offer up their sufferings, encouraged the man to write on Christ in the prison, the woman to put her love into her drawings. A couple arrived in Paris with little money and started life in a miserable room. He set his Jocists to work to find a lodging, gave the wife secretarial employment, encouraged both to have their meals in his kitchen with him. Another couple had their electric light cut off: he gave them a packet of candles, saying, " These were given to me for the chapel: use them to light your home. It does not change their purpose, for a home is also a sanctuary."

He would watch over a long engagement and prepare the two for their marriage, he would bless first the betrothal and then the marriage itself. " Yes," he wrote to one girl, " you can spend a day in prayer to get ready for your final ' yes '. But don't get yourself all worried. God is smiling on your love. He is happy over it."

" When the great change in my life came," writes a young man, " and I met my fiancée, he was marvellous. . . .

" I couldn't tell you all he did for us. Every young family had a share in him. He taught me how to love greatly, generously, totally. He was really happy when he saw two people in love. Love was the great dream of his whole life, and all his work spoke of it. He betrothed us and he married us. Ours was the last marriage he blessed. One day, December 6, 1943, he came to our nest and gave us a réco. It was very simple and it was wonderful."

I possess a villainously executed copy of one of these récos—done in purple and black and pale grey copying ink in Godin's handwriting. Patchy and illegible as it is, it is a really amazing performance. He begins with the Holy Trinity: the Son the

Thought of the Father and that Thought a Person: the Spirit the love, the total self-giving of Father to Son and Son to Father. Christ's love for His Church and His self-gift. What should be our return of love?

He leads them on to the thought of the gift of themselves to one another, of the spiritual life to be led together, of the relation of husband and wife in the details of daily life, of their relation to God. The meditations are interspersed with questionnaires, some for the husband, some for the wife, some for both together: to be worked over and prayed about.

Godin wrote a book, *Le Christ dans la Construction du Foyer*, and collaborated in another in both of which there are passages of deep, delicate understanding of the relation between flesh and spirit.

" Like the earth itself sex has its rhythm drawn from the deepest sources of life. . . . Between the love of body and of soul is a union that cannot be broken. . . . The love of sense would soon fade if the spiritual soul did not bring to it a new meaning. But the spirit would not be so rich if it had not hearkened to the mysterious world of fleshly feelings. Thus, one sustaining and enriching the other and in turn strengthened by it, the rhythm of the life of flesh keeps harmony with that even deeper and more mysterious rhythm of the heart and of the love of souls.

" It seems to me that here we touch a vital point in the question of continence. It is possible when the soul dilates, not when it narrows."

This mysterious being thus created by God is created for a high destiny and it is in the flesh that he is called upon to fulfil it. Nay, more, God Himself took human flesh at the Incarnation and our human lives must be a continuation today of Christ's Incarnation. To this thought he returns constantly.

" We have all of us to continue the Incarnation: this is the very function of the Church. And the Incarnation is to put into flesh the divine life, to put the divine into the human, the material. . . .

" Apart from a special vocation (priestly or religious) the Christian should not run away from what is material, what is of the flesh. But he should try to put the divine into it. He will act like any other man, but he will do it as a son of God.

" The more generous your life, the more you put of the love of God and of a beautiful human love into all your acts, even the least of them, the more you will help the growth of Christ's Mystical Body.

" For all your good acts are a part of you as you are a part of that Mystical Body. The wife should love her husband in Christ, and in her her husband should see God's tabernacle, should see the bearer of a wonderful mission: the giving of children to their Saviour."

And then comes that touch of tenderness when we see him speaking to Riton and Paulette, or Dédé and Madeleine, to his own children:

" No, never get accustomed to one another: never look at one another with the eyes of the world: look at one another with God's eyes. You are so much more beautiful as He sees you. You are so much greater."

Probably nothing in the whole tragedy of the proletariat troubled Abbé Godin more deeply than the loss of the ideals of marriage and the terrible conditions under which young couples had to make their beginnings. What had they seen at home, what had they learned from the cinema or the radio, what entry was there for Christian ideas into their minds? Only this—that God had made them, that their love itself would open their hearts to His Spirit: that especially at this moment the priest would find them ready as never before, as perhaps never again.

But to act anywhere an agent must be present in some fashion. Among the proletarian masses priests were present in no fashion. Then, too, as will be seen fully in his own words, it was not merely work for individuals that he felt was needed, but the foundation of Christian communities among the proletariat who could not be fitted into the existent parishes. What was to be done about it?

The same question was being asked by other priests throughout the country, and it was in relation to the countryside as well as the towns that a practical answer had already begun to be given. In 1937 a book appeared by M. Bettencourt with a preface by Cardinal Suhard, then Archbishop of Rheims. The author urged: (1) A seminary for home missions to train priests who should specialise in the apostolate of conversion. (2) A rural Society of the Propagation of the Faith to allow of a new evangelisation of the pagan country areas. Even earlier Canon Féron, national chaplain of the Ligue Agricole Chrétienne, had made a similar suggestion to the Episcopate, but it was only in July 1941 that at their Assembly the Cardinals and Archbishops decided to set such a seminary on foot.

It is believed by all concerned that Sainte Thérèse herself drew the seminary to Lisieux. Patron of foreign missions, she was no less concerned in the Mission de France. The scheme was confided to the Society of Saint Sulpice, and that September Canon Augros found himself lodged at Carmel itself— alone with his hopes, and the prayers and hospitality of the nuns. From January to July 1942 he managed, despite zonal boundaries, to visit sixty dioceses, and in October thirty priests and seminarists had gathered around four professors for their first spiritual reading. " A new page has begun in the history of the Church of France. It will become whatever we make of it."

By 1943 the first missionaries were being sent out and the number of students rose to sixty. By preference men were at first taken who had completed their philosophy. They learn theology with a special application to missionary work. They operate in teams alike for study and manual work as it is in teams that they will later go out. They are given more liberty and personal responsibility than in most seminaries: all the studies are related to the work of evangelisation. Every man has as part of his training what is called a " stade " as a farm labourer, or some other sort of workman. This lasts from a few months to a year or more and is designed to teach them to know and love those among whom they are to work. Even this *stade* is usually made in groups. The final shape of the work is not that of an itinerant missionary: they go out to build Christian communities inside pagan areas. The stress is on building these communities more than on individual conversions. The seminary is inter-diocesan, but when a team is assigned to a particular diocese it comes under the Bishop of that diocese. That they are seculars, not religious, is strongly insisted on.

While the aim and ideals of the seminary are very clear they still view their techniques as experimental in the sense that they remain constantly open to new ideas and developments that may prove valuable for the adaptation of means to the great end of re-Christianising France.

It was in the same year, 1943, that Abbé Godin began, says Doctor Tremolière, to make of the problems of *France, Pays de Mission?* the very centre of his life and of his thought. Cardinal Suhard had asked of him and of a fellow Jocist chaplain, Abbé Daniel, a report on the conditions of the proletariat in relation to the Church. Abbé Daniel, himself a striking personality, only wanted when I visited him to talk of Godin and to read aloud pages from his books. But he broke off presently to describe how they had collaborated. Working in two different districts of Paris, each man threw in his own personal experiences; Abbé Daniel furnished the over-all statistics and Abbé Godin the sociological reflexions.

The report accepted by the Cardinal was published with his authorisation under the title *France, Pays de Mission?*

As Jocist chaplains, both men continued to believe in the methods of Catholic Action as the best and most effective for the Church of today. But both felt, as the book shows, that it had become in large areas too narrowly parochial. Canon Cardijn had said, " Our first interest lies in those who do not belong to us," but in practice many groups were totally out of touch with " those who do not belong to us ". A new missionary orientation was needed.

It would seem also that among the Jocist chaplains themselves were two schools of thought as to the spiritual orientation of the movement. Godin writes in an undated note:

" I understood the J.O.C. in principle but not in practice.

" At the beginning I did not want to make too Christian a movement of it, agreeing with Abbé X., and I never completely recovered from this mistake. That with my own lukewarmness was the cause of my set-back. . . .

" I have not been priestly enough."

From the missionary angle the indispensable action of the laity was incomplete without a deeper compenetration by the clergy than had yet been attempted. The Jocists were the advance guard—and the advance guard is in danger unless the army is close behind it. The whole Church must become missionary.

"What struck me most in the whole business," says Doctor Tremolière, " was the degree to which Abbé Godin started from a *lived experience* carrying the problem within him in anguish and building up his thought *from day to day* through a series of experiences. He never started from what is commonly called a ' critical study '—a thing that he loathed. I remember one evening showing him a plan for such a study of our bourgeois Catholic Action. He demolished it harshly in a single phrase, ' That sort of work has never built anything.' "

He wanted to learn from the experiences of others, and in 1942 he had asked the Mission de France to receive him as a pupil, going down week by week to join the priests' study circles. For while the majority at the seminary are students, a certain number of priests go there to do a year's theology with a special application to their future missionary life. Into these study groups, says the superior, Godin brought far more than he received. " I observed in him," he continues, " a number of qualities so opposite as to be disconcerting until one grasped the resultant harmony. Are not rich personalities made up of contrasts? He appeared for instance extremely bold, revolutionary, upsetting all conventions, traditions, set forms. Yet at other times he seemed timid (and he was), prudent (he was that too), capable of considerate kindnesses that only a very noble and very affectionate character would think of."

A vivid impression of Henri Godin was given me by Abbé Lorenzo, now curé of Saint Hippolyte at Choisy, who had known him at Lisieux and who confirms the remarkable harmony in Godin of qualities usually opposed. Deeply serious, thoughtful, *silent* (this man who yet so needed, as Abbé Guérin says, to pour out his thoughts), possessed of great self-command, great boldness, his ascendancy over other men was, says Abbé Lorenzo, amazing—not only over his own militants, but also over priests. And this is almost surprising.

Talking to many of the priests who knew him best, one gets much the same reactions as from the lads. " What impression did he first make on you? " I asked one after another, receiving the answer, " None at all. He kept in the background," or, " He passed unnoticed," or, " At first I thought him an oddity." Sometimes the contact was swift: on a first meeting Abbé Depierre said to him, " This is the first time I have met a priest who was a real priest." With others it was never made at all. When one sees impeccably neat priests in well-brushed clothes one realises that Godin's exterior must at first have put them off. The dirty soutane that reached hardly below his knees, " You could make soup from it," a boy told me; the unwashed hands, " The Lavabo was strictly necessary," said a man who had served his Mass. For Abbé Daniel he had a perpetual joke —that they should seal their friendship by washing their hands in the same water. I do not think Abbé Daniel would have enjoyed it, yet he came to adore Godin.

It was slowly for the most part but surely that he entered into their lives as a great experience.

" It is my impression," says a university professor, " that, at any rate until he died, a good many of his brethren and former schoolfellows did not understand him, misled perhaps by the fact that his mysticism lay so deep within him. . . . He brought great wealth to me by teaching me self-devotion and directing me towards a more genuine and more communal apostolate. He made me grasp how far a priest's self-oblation must go. I sometimes told him I could never lead a life like his: then he tried to give me the idea by his way of acting that such devotedness was great fun."

"He made it his business", says a fellow chaplain of the J.O.C., "to lead us to the discovery of our vocation of every day. One always left him feeling light and confident, seeing things more clearly and filled with an astonishing spirit of generosity . . ."

Père Maydieu, O.P. (of the *Vie Intellectuelle*), speaks of him as "the priest whose entire life and outlook asked of his brother priests the one question of overwhelming importance: ' What about you, are you wholly and entirely a priest? '

"The invocation that came from the heart of a militant, ' Père Godin pray for us ', is not overbold. Let me add, ' Gain for us the grace to be such priests as you '."

Canon Cardijn sees Godin, like Ste. Thérèse, spending his eternity doing good upon earth "as chaplain of a heavenly Jocist section, that supreme missionary section that will inspire all those on earth, those of Paris, of France, of the world-wide J.O.C. of the future. . . . May we be worthy of him".

"Under an appearance of amiable joviality," says Canon Tiberghien of Lille, "he hid a spirit of renunciation and a life of poverty which one could not suggest as model to anyone who had not the graces of a special divine call."

And, often though Godin insisted on the human side in relation to his boys and girls, he felt as a priest and indicated strongly to the canon the "necessity of passing rapidly through the human to reach the divine. When I said, ' Well, and how can we pass through the human to the divine? ' I received this answer, one of the last things he said to me, and which all my life will be my Viaticum, ' The path from the human to the divine goes through Calvary '."

" S.O.S.

" Dear Doctor,

" It isn't going too well. All the same I don't want to die without doctor's permission. It would be annoying to the Faculty, so I want to bring you my poor carcase to be overhauled.

" There's no hurry for a day or two, but I can't work at all any more.

" Very cordially—for my heart is still functioning,

" H. Godin."

Of course he didn't stop working; instead, as we have seen, he was planning a new creation—a mission for proletarian Paris. After receiving the report on conditions, Cardinal Suhard had decided to call on Abbé Godin to bring this into being. At first they had thought simply of a Paris branch of the Mission de France, but on further consideration a separate society appeared preferable. The Mission de France is for the whole country, rural as well as urban. The Mission de Paris is for Paris alone. The one is missionary for all pagans, the other is directed specifically towards the proletariat. The one is under the entire hierarchy, the other under the Archbishop of Paris only. While both are highly experimental, the Mission de France tends to work within a parochial framework, that of Paris is absolutely outside it. The Mission de France, until the creation several years later of its branch of women auxiliaries, was purely clerical, that of Paris had layfolk from the very beginning as an integral part of its—I had almost written organisation, but such a word as entity or even organism is to be preferred.

For Abbé Godin's strength and weakness alike lay in his attitude towards organisation. Obviously the thing must exist: he was no good at it: let those engage in it who were: for his part he was inclined to smile and pass it by. If you will not organise, his critics might have said, everything will fall to pieces. And Godin might have answered: not if it is alive.

The Cardinal had asked for an experienced parish priest in the Mission and Abbé Godin rejoiced at securing the Abbé Hollande as its superior. To more than one person he said that his own work was finished, that now he could say his *Nunc dimittis*. To others it seemed that he was only at the start of a rich, full ministry. True, he had done much. But he was not yet thirty-eight, he was growing in stature every year.

It was December 1943, and it was decided to hold a month of study and prayer in preparation for the new venture. After a week at Combes-la-ville they moved to Lisieux. The Cardinal had laid down two general principles: that the Mission was designed entirely for the conversion of the heathen and was an extension of Catholic Action, but also, " Its indirect end is to show the Christian community that it must take up a new attitude. A shock is needed." A delicate matter to produce a shock without being shocking! So Abbé Godin gathered canon lawyers and theologians into his conference. He had, he knew, to watch himself, for he loved to give a shock and did not the least mind becoming shocking in pious eyes or what is sometimes called an offence to pious ears.

At this conference, we are told, Abbé Godin for the first time in his life showed the depth and width of his own theological learning. Usually modest and retiring on this head he discussed the questions he had raised with an eloquence and wealth of reference that amazed the scholars he had assembled.

To a layman, an intimate friend of Abbé Godin's, I once complained that people were using his ideas without acknowledgement. He answered, " What does it matter as long as the ideas get about? " And I remembered how Saint Thérèse had chosen as a supreme practice of poverty allowing others to take possession of ideas that are yours.

Godin went even further, but with him it is hard to tell how much was humility, how much an exercise of his rather peculiar idea of a joke. " In his quest for poverty, " says Abbé Lelièvre, " he wanted to be poorly thought of and he felt he had played a good trick when some learned personage abounding in intellectual lights dismissed him as a nitwit or a fanatic."

Such men, says Abbé Hua (national chaplain of the Mouvement Populaire des Familles), saw nothing but the spelling mistakes " of this priest whose culture was so wide and so deep . . . [who was in fact] a first-class theologian who during his studies at the Institut Catholique had read St. Augustine in Migne's Patrology from end to end, steeped in moral theology . . . a skilful psychologist . . . an artist and lover of the beautiful."

Abbé Michonneau notes his power of thinking on command, of assembling all the elements of a problem in a swift synthesis and then breaking them down to help his interlocutor, of getting the wavelength of another man. " His mind, too, never stopped its work . . . his odd moments, his comings and goings were never empty."

" His rich personality, " says another confrère, " united the mind of a philosopher with that amazing power of attention to the smallest details of the concrete."

Many to whom I talked in Paris asked me: " Have you seen the outlines of the Conferences at Lisieux? " and appeared to attach immense importance to them. They talked of those days as profoundly affecting their own lives and as significant in the history of the Church. At long last the document has come into my hands. Like everything connected with Abbé Godin, its appearance is against it. He probably multigraphed it himself, so hard it is to read—lines omitted or smudged out, whole pages in almost invisible ink, words altered and misplaced, the pages not numbered and assembled in the wrong order, retreat notes mixed up with those of the discussions. But there is matter for months of fruitful meditation, and as one reads and re-reads them one experiences something of what Canon Glorieux has dared to call a new Pentecost.

Men had come together who had often separately been agonising over the same great problem. *France, Pays de Mission?* is described by several of them as a " bombshell " for the general public, but for them it was but the publicising of a sad truth already too well known. And now they were met to face it more fully and to pray and work with new light and strength.

I had already been greatly impressed by the attitude of the Mission de France towards this new mission. Not only was there no petty jealousy, but Canon Augros threw open his seminary for the discussions and brought to them all the wealth of his own knowledge and experience.

And he, as founder and superior of the Mission de France, insists strongly on the contribution furnished to his own work by the founder of this new mission, a contribution in which as time went on he found an ever richer content.

" 1. He helped us to define our general lines of action. Missionary work everywhere must consist in making Christ and the Church become incarnate in true human communities, whether this be among the masses, peasant or proletarian, among the bourgeosie or university students. Everywhere we are seeking a solution for the same problem.

" 2. He opened to the Mission de France the road it had been vainly seeking for eighteen months towards the working masses. From its very foundation by the Assembly of Cardinals and Archbishops, the Mission de France had been intended to be not rural only but universal. It had therefore been obliged to explore roads in all directions. Unless we had met Abbé Godin we should not yet have fully discovered our road into the world of the worker.

" In the history of the Mission de France a very high place must be given to the Abbé Godin."

55

Among the subjects discussed were the theology of Catholic
Action, position of a lay evangelist in the Church, Church and
State, the place of prophecy and its subjection to the Magis-
terium, the direction of the young, the requirements of the
proletarian world, education of the affections and its utilisation
for Christian conquest (here we see a distinctively Godin touch:
for him sex-education implied primarily the affections). The
history of the Church was studied: her expansion, her beginnings in pagan lands, past and present experiments, missionary
history of the last twenty years. A profounder theology was
sought in talks on Christ the Perfect Man and Christ the Man
of Sorrows, on the foundations of an apostolic priesthood, on
Our Lady, poverty, simplicity, and on the teaching of doctrine.
God's transcendence of creation, as well as His immanence in
creation, Christ's unity with the Father, are taken as models for
the apostle: to be close to God is the only way of bringing God
close to man. Redemptive suffering is deeply contemplated in
Christ and in Mary. " Jesus, above all, received from His
Mother a body through which He could suffer. And this is
His first reason for loving His Mother, that she enabled Him
to suffer. And it is because of His great love for her that He
asks her to suffer with Him."

Poverty is one suffering that is an absolute condition for a
fruitful mission. " The apostolate calls for greater poverty
than the religious life." " The apostle must never be *installé
dans la vie*." This thought keeps recurring. While the parish
priest living among real Christians has the right to claim a
living from his parishioners, the missionary must never appear
" to have settled down in this world ".

Under the heading of Simplicity comes a delightful paragraph
that is pure Godin: " The spirit should be wholly illuminated
by the truth: the most direct way of reaching this is contemplation: this is why contemplatives stay so young. Order can
only come into life through this fierce love of truth, no com-
promise with bluff, no truck with wuffling or unreality. ' Est-
est, Non-non '."

Among the most interesting outlines are those which concern religious education—and they are cheering to a Catholic Evidence Guild speaker as bringing testimony from another land that our own general line has been a right one. In " The Position of a Lay Evangelist " it is laid down that " in the degree to which a Christian lives his faith mystically he must live by it intellectually too ". To bear witness is not enough. There must also be a power to *show* truths to minds. And he likes to call the special grace of a catechist's " state of life " a " charism " bestowed on him for the sake of the whole community.

Teaching has been, since the Reformation and Counter-Reformation, set in a mould of apologetics and argument. Catholics are injured by the study circle method, they become disputatious, with an inferior type of scholasticism. The Bible is used only as an arsenal of negative arguments and has become a closed book to most; they don't look at the great religious movement it unfolds (e.g. we never read the Acts and therefore do not understand the Church).

Theologically we are more occupied in proving (even to those who have the faith already) than in exploring the truth, getting deep into the Christian mystery. (Godin often used to say, " You can talk to anyone, even the simplest, about the Trinity.")

The negative nature of our teaching is shown in most of the lessons in morality and the effort to impose it. " Teach dogma and practice will follow." Virtue is taught by telling people what they mustn't do—e.g. purity is not shown in its own splendour but as " a catalogue of negative prescriptions ". Too often one virtue is emphasised through fear of its opposite : charity through fear of strength, humility through fear of courage, obedience through fear of responsibility.

We must learn to offer Christ's message in all its power: no need to destroy first all the difficulties that may arise (e.g. we speak of the problem of evil as though God had to justify Himself).

The Church appears dull and bourgeois, especially to the young, because her mystical resources have not been offered them. Christianity involves a *mystique* and we must not be afraid to preach it. The mysteries are a Revelation. Faith is a power of illumination and elevation: grace a nature with healing and uplifting powers. Much of this we can teach through the Church's history. " We can only arrive at the Church as the Mystical Body through the reality of her temporal existence, just as in order to reach the Word we begin by laying hold on Christ as Man. The history of the Church is itself theology."

Godin's reactions were, his biographer tells us, very animated: he showed his dislike of conformity, " one is almost tempted to say his anti-clericalism ", pretty freely. " We must always be ready for new methods," he said. " Finality is inhuman. Organisation kills unless it leaves room for life to spring up." But to Abbé Hua, national chaplain of the Mouvement Populaire des Familles, he said several times, " My gift is to plough the furrow quite straight without swerving to right or left. It is possible that I shall fail: indeed it is probable. But the furrow will be traced in the right direction. Others will arise to take up the work where I have left it."

And with all his " reactions " he did produce a remarkable balance of opposites—fighting at once against a religion too deeply implicated in matter and thus losing its *mystique* or too remote from daily life and thus ineffective in elevating it. " Guiding lines," says Glorieux, " were sought for, bases of action corresponding with the guidings of psychology and the results of experiments already attempted."

How straight the furrow was, how intelligent the lines he drew, I had hardly realised until I saw these papers and was able to relate them with the developments that have followed.

Cardinal Suhard came down to Lisieux to bless the new venture and send forth its missionaries with full authority. The great month ended with a High Mass at midnight which was, by Godin's request, that of Our Lady of Victories. It was in Our Lady's hands that, in a very simple formula, the priests of this new mission laid the offering of their work among the heathen of their own land. Abbé Godin had drawn up the formula, but a formula could not reveal the ardent love of Our Lady, the trust in her that inspired his prayers. He had told her before he was a priest that Saint John Bosco had asked too little in begging her for a thousand places in Heaven. " With absolute trust, I ask you for ten thousand."

She was the Mother of his proletarian children, the Shepherdess of the sheep—and he was her rough, uncouth sheepdog:

" To you, most loving Mother, Jesus has entrusted His flock. Your sheep in the great meadow of the world cannot be numbered. And your chosen flock is that of the slums and alleys because there are more unhappy sinners among them, and, above all, because they have made you weep most frequently.

" Around you, gentle Shepherdess, are gathered a few white, unspotted sheep (oh! so few!), trembling and dismayed by all the noise that is made to frighten them away.

" And in the distance, in great workmen's blocks and flats and in the crowded streets are the immense flock of sheep lost or run away and roaming through the woods.

" They don't even know that the good Shepherdess is looking for them, is loving them.

" And every day the wolves make ravages upon them, so great and so many that nearly all are lost. . . ."

Our Lady has begged Our Lord for helpers, and he wants to do his best as her sheepdog. He describes himself in this function:

" He barks a lot. He goes eagerly wherever he is sent.

" He eats what he is given without a fuss and lies down to sleep wherever he happens to be.

" When he is too slow, clumsy, and awkward, and the sheep run away from him into the fields and the woods where the wolf

will get them, take up your crook, swift and beautiful Shepherdess, and fly to his help.

" Your big sheepdog only wants to obey, to pass unnoticed,
and if you like, when he is very tired, to rest near you for a few
minutes and beg you for a smile or a caress. But only if you
like.

" And later on in heaven a little corner near you, oh so tiny,
lying in the middle of the flock now all safely gathered in
forever."

Several times, as the conference proceeded, Godin repeated
his conviction that he was no longer needed and also his high
hopes for the future of the Mission. For the Holy Ghost was
manifestly with it.

On Saturday, January 15, all returned to Paris and on Sunday
Abbé Godin gave a Recollection for his young couples. As
he said Goodnight to Abbé Depierre, who was sharing his
flat, he said once more, " It's a miracle the way everything has
turned out: now I can vanish. The Mission can do without
me."

It was mid-January and the weather was bitter in the Rue
Ganneron. For his gas stove the abbé had lately substituted
a coal one. He was suffering from headaches, but it did not
occur to either his doctor or himself that they were caused by
fumes from the stove. It was found afterwards that the chimney
was completely blocked.

Monday morning the Mission was to be launched, but on
Monday morning Henri Godin was found lying dead on his
bed, asphyxiated by the fumes from the stove, the room full
of smoke, the bed half burned and his feet scorched by his
electric heater.

" He went suddenly," said one of the Jocists, " as if he were
answering a call. It was the only way for him. He went the
way he lived, simply, all alone, without saying good-bye or
giving any final instructions. The first few days we were
shattered, like the Apostles shut up in the Cenacle after the

death of the great Workman. And we cried for a long time. That's not just a phrase: we really wept; we wept bitter tears. We mourned him as you mourn a father."

They mourned, but they were comforted. The boy who had come home from Germany on leave, and ran up the stairs to find his friend dead—" *Coincidence cette perm* [Leave]? No, my God, I thank you for having been there for his funeral which was a revelation. . . . And now, back in exile I can say to myself, ' He is not dead, he is more than ever present, watching over his son who will work himself to death if need be to carry out the Mission you have made him discover. No, Abbé, I will never let you down '."

And then there was the girl who could not forgive God for his death. She tells quite simply how she went up to the little room and then something began to happen. " I wasn't alone. Christ was with me and was beginning His work."

For four days an endless procession moved down the steep street, climbed the three storeys and knelt to pray beside their priest. Cardinal Suhard came, and most of the notables of Catholic Paris. At night as men and girls left their work the procession became denser and the crowd overflowed the little room.

All night for four nights Jocists watched by the bed. " At half-past one we had Mass in Père Godin's study where he was lying so near us . . . that Mass was for me the most beautiful, the most deeply realised, the most lived, the best understood. And I was happy, for I felt that Père Godin had begun to work on me. In a little while, in a few moments even, I wasn't the same girl. I began to make resolutions on the spot because I knew very well that with the help of Père Godin I should have less difficulty in keeping them . . ."

The Requiem, with four priests giving Communion to a vast crowd at past midday, was a spontaneous expression of grief and of triumph. Boys and girls went on to their work knowing it would be evening before they could get more than the bit of bread they were carrying to eat on the way. And Godin was buried as he had chosen to live, among the workers in the vast cemetery of Pantin in a poor man's grave.

"He is not dead," said one of his children, "he is more alive among us than ever. Now he is more powerful than ever. We should be joyous as he was. He has given us the helm to hold. Hold fast, for he is guiding our ship from up there."

Part II

FRANCE A MISSIONARY LAND?

By HENRI GODIN and YVAN DANIEL

I. WHAT THE PROBLEM IS

Is France a Missionary Country ?

WHEN we are morally challenged by a serious and complex problem that may upset our lives we are only too apt to discover a solution that liberates our conscience and banishes the intrusive challenge, yet is purely academic.

We all observed the diminishing Christianity of France. Our peace was disturbed: we even began to fear that positive paganism was close upon us.

Then we found the formula: " France is a missionary country."

We repeated this, printed it, preached it, embodied it in reports, proclaimed it at Congresses. All this has soothed us: after all (we feel) we are clearly alive to the grave problems of the day, we are not the men to shirk them. . . .

Christian Areas, Non-practising Areas of a Christian Culture, Missionary Areas

It would be amazing if so general, so simplified an assertion could be taken literally: and it would be a pity if it were to hold us back from a deeper study of our actual religious condition— above all, a pity if it absolved us from action.

If I went to Villedieu-la-Blouère I should find a township of fifteen hundred inhabitants (one-third peasants, two-thirds workers in shoe factories). All the girls practise their religion: only a very few young men do not; family night prayers are customary and there are quite a number of fine large families. Who would dare to call this mission country?

But at Bac d'Asnières, at Clichy (numbering two or three thousand souls), few children make their first Communion,

65

none at all persevere later, not a single man goes to Church and for several years the Jocists have been trying in vain to establish a section. Here indeed we are in an absolutely pagan area.

Neither of these places represents the whole of France. There are villages more Christian than the former, while in the region of Paris there are zones well known as even worse than the latter. And there are many intermediate areas, especially all those regions *where a Christian mentality* still subsists deep down despite the absence of religious practices.

From the missionary viewpoint we would divide France—very roughly, of course, for all such divisions must be more or less unsatisfactory when we are dealing with a living organism —into regions falling into three categories:

(1) *Regions Christian in mind, culture and worship,* such as Villedieu. There are missionary enthusiasts who try to prove that even these villages need re-Christianising. They explain that religion is growing more and more superficial, that Christianity enters less and less into people's lives and is progressively ostracised from their institutions, that factory life there, as elsewhere, is degrading and demoralising, that a population incapable of self-defence is being subjected daily to the pagan assaults that are affecting the nation as a whole— the Press, the cinema, the radio. You cannot, they say, save from invasion a town lost in the midst of a conquered country.

We fully share their fears: these areas are in danger, the alarm must be sounded. As fully as the rest, more urgently even, there is need to rejuvenate them through Catholic Action. But still, we do not think they can actually be called missionary territory.

Is it not the universal fate of Christianity to be under attack from within by lukewarmness and formality when not from without by the forces of evil?

The " wonderful Christianity " of the Middle Ages—talked of so often (perhaps a trifle naïvely) as the thousand years' reign of Christ—quite certainly suffered from all these difficulties, was aware of all these inadequacies: with one exception: there was not the enveloping atmosphere that breathes from pagan institutions.

But was the religion always fully personal? Did not the Christian atmosphere, the tradition, often carry along the individual despite all his defects and all his weaknesses?

We would rather, from a missionary viewpoint, put in our first category those French parishes that are still living and very active Christian communities, even though they are being mined from within. These regions are in danger of collapsing if not infused with the new blood of a personal, intensely-lived Christianity.

(2) *Areas where the culture and civilisation remain Christian but where Christian practice is restricted to small groups* more or less fervent and tending to live shut in among themselves.

Territorially this represents by far the greater part of France. Apart from a few dioceses it must be considered as the melancholy background of a tapestry, relieved here and there by the Christian areas which show on it like patterns embroidered with colours more or less rich and of varying extent.

Full religious practice, entire obedience to the divine law, confidence in our mother the Church and childlike trust in her have become rare—all this has been emphasised time and time again with the backing of statistics. Setting aside the great cities, of the adult population of France only one-tenth practises the Faith. I know all this: and yet I do not think all these parishes can be classed as missionary areas.

We see the new things—the radio, the cinema, the newspapers—coming from the great cities and bringing a pagan spirit that is slowly eating away the soul of France. But we must look also at all that is left of habits, traditions, age-long institutions, fundamental ideas, ancestral judgements—all Christian, all still to some extent operative.

No, our political leaders know, as we know, that there still remains in these areas a *Christian basis*, a *Christian civilisation*.

Only compare the outlook of these so-called pagans with that of the pagans of old Rome and we sense the difference. If you have had dealings with real pagans you appreciate how much of Christ's teaching is still left in France.

These people only come to Mass on great feasts, perhaps even only at great moments in their lives, but they do come. They come impelled by a sick and enfeebled faith, buried beneath the dust of superstitions, pushed away into their subconscious, but still alive. And its life is a tough one, for it has endured almost without assistance all the batteries turned against it for the past century. Young men, even some young women, lose their purity, but *they know* that impurity is a sin and they condemn it as a sin. They commit plenty of sins— but it is a characteristic of Christian lands where the law is known that it is also much sinned against. These are the sins " of Christian sinners ", as Péguy puts it—and a " Christian sinner " is much more than a pagan.

We must emphasise the values of hard work, of the family virtues that still stand unshaken—of all the Christian virtues that remain: only latent perhaps, but creating an atmosphere and a culture that still is Christian.

Parishes in the first category might be compared to a beautiful house, kept in good order even though the trained eye might discover menacing cracks and crevices that call for repairs if the house is to stand in years to come.

The second sort of parish is more like an old French village, solidly built out of vast stones that could defy the ages. It falls into ruins, or perhaps a war has passed over it. The roofs have fallen in, the windows are broken, the doors have disappeared, the paths are a mass of thistles and the borders of dandelions. To go through the village gives you a heartache and you think of it as dead. But no : a team of young workers gets going; the roofs are broken down, but the houses are there, the roads are there, the gardens are there. Give them six months or a year and you will see a lovely little village on the hillside, active and joyous.

Of course to bring back life to a Christian community sunk in a lethargic sleep takes longer than a year. We know that this broken-down state is very serious—that, left unremedied, it grows worse day by day; a decline is not an illness that can last forever; if no cure is found, hope vanishes. In the same way, the longer you wait to rebuild a village the more likely you are to arrive too late and find yourself obliged to sweep away the vestiges of the past that have become unusable.

Yet if the parish priest of one of these villages were to accuse us of too much optimism, he would show that he has never had to face a really pagan world, where *everything* has to be done, where there is nothing to build on, where all the deepest powers of men's souls have been vitiated, all their desires and cravings turned towards false gods.

We do not think that these regions are in danger of being easily captured by any positive philosophy of paganism that may come along. Their Christianity is weak, and in the struggle with a false mysticism, young and dynamic, it would in time be certainly defeated, but it is strongly rooted. It would hold its ground like a cathedral in a bombardment: it would be destroyed, but only after a long time and repeated blows. And there are many unconscious Christians, so that the work of reconstruction may still be relatively quick.

(3) *Pagan areas. Missionary areas.* These constitute the third category of the districts of France. Returning to the metaphor of a tapestry, we can only look upon them as holes in the fabric, for from a Christian viewpoint nothing at all is left. They are vast rents in the map of France indicating entire lost areas, or smaller holes where the large towns should be. The rents represent country districts where no Christian tradition is left—love of money has devoured it, politics have ravaged it, absence of the clergy has let it all die. There are, we are told, rural " cantons " which no longer exist on the religious map of France. The rural problem is not that with which we are concerned, but M. l'Abbé Boulard, in his *L'Art d'être Curé de*

Campagne, has plotted the ground in exactly the same fashion as we have, showing that his problem, if not identical, is at least parallel with ours. Parallel, yes, identical, no.

For in truth we can find only analogies and not clear similarity between situations as different as those of the urban proletariat, the paganised peasantry and the bourgeois pagan world. (For there is also a bourgeois paganism, flooding in upon the middle classes, which has not been sufficiently studied and which is eating through the protective armour of our society.)

But to face our problem seriously, to get at the absolute religious reality we are discussing, we must separate these categories. The peasant is profoundly different from the townsman. The peasant reflects, he draws life from the deep places of his soul, from his subconscious, from a millenary past. He becomes a pagan more slowly than the townsman, more painfully. The remains of the old religious tradition always mean something for him, something deep, usually something solid. First Communion, marriage, religious burial, are all acts of faith binding him to religion.

These same things are for the townsman almost without significance, they are merely conventional gestures, depending on the part of the country he comes from, the society he lives in, and a mass of surrounding circumstances. Your townsman lives on the surface of things. The legacy of his past is buried deep, never to rise again perhaps—or at least only under extraordinary circumstances. This is the great lack, the great unhappiness of townsmen; they are men uprooted from the past, with no help from their race or their surroundings . . . And we know how poor and little a man becomes, left alone in time and in space.

To return to Clichy and the towns of which it is a type. No Christian life here, no Christian culture either, indeed no culture of any kind. There is a veneer of " civilisation," very remote from the kind of culture Mgr. Bruno de Solages has defined as " that which enables man to discover his place in the universe and to give a meaning to his life ".

He continues : " A man of culture is a man who after sufficient (sometimes lengthy) consideration can weigh and measure all that passes before him: a man who can give everything its proper value, recognising that there is a hierarchy, a certain proportion in the various elements of human knowledge. Such a man need not be a mine of information. A delver into knowledge, if he does not know how to order and arrange it, is learned but not cultured. On the other hand, a man may have wide fields of ignorance and still be a cultured man."

In this region and in all like it, whether a man inhabits the elegant garden city or the vast workman's dwelling, he knows nothing of whence he comes, whither he is going, why he is on this earth. He has no reason for living, no guiding principles, no scale of values. Nor do you find among such people that basis of Christian values that elsewhere helps you to reach many Christians even though they are unconscious that they are Christians. Even that natural morality is gone, which philosophers and great men can find written in their own minds but which the little ones can learn only from the Gospel.

Yes, here we are indeed in missionary country. If on certain sides we are not so low (no positive paganism with the rites and morals which support it), in other respects our position is a worse one: the backward people we call savages have kept in their age-old tradition something of primitive revelation. Here we find nothing, sheer emptiness . . . with civilisation superimposed.

II. WHAT IS A MISSION?

A MISSION is the renewal of Christ's act in taking flesh and coming on earth to save us; a mission is the telling of the Good News to men who do not know it. Both in its etymological sense and according to common speech, the word "mission" signifies this sending forth of Truth and of Light to men and societies that lack them.

A missionary goes where nothing yet exists: he is sent to establish Christ's Church in some human society, he is about to *start* a Christian community. Thus when a canon of Turcoing is sent as a bishop to La Rochelle he cannot be called a missionary: he is a pastor. He is going to rule over a flock, uniting, of course, the urge to win new souls with the cares of administration.

But a missionary is setting out to found a Christian community in a country or in a society where none yet exists. Thus there can be no question of missionaries inside a Christian country—even when, for example, the parish priest of Villedieu sets out to win the eight or ten apostates of his parish. In areas non-practising but still Christian in culture, the missionary *spirit* can find a place: the Christian community must grow, must spread—yet here, too, is a Church already in existence asking for a pastor. And it is interesting to note that men who do not themselves practise often demand a parish priest, sometimes quite energetically.

We must not, of course, think of communities only in terms of territorial divisions. In a fervent New York parish a mission for coloured people may be urgently needed; in India one caste may have its Christian community while in the same area another caste must still be thought of in terms of a mission.

WHAT IS A MISSION?

What must never be forgotten is that the missionary aposto-late lies not in creating individual Christians in the midst of a pagan world, for by this method nothing but a small élite can be hoped for. Rather it consists in creating Christian communities: every human community should be a Christian community, existent or in the making. If it is in the making, at least a section of the whole is a Christian community, and it goes forth to win over the rest. In this section the Church has taken flesh.

Contemporary individualism has misled us in this business. We have to recall the fact that the universal Church is the grouping, in a profound and mysterious reality and also in a human organism, of all the individual Churches that tend to spring up in every human group.

All these individual Churches, in each human society, in every centre of life, are indispensable: they alone can create an atmosphere that supports and carries along the ordinary man. For man is a social being; to live fully he must enter into the give and take of human solidarity; if he does not accept this law of his existence he will not fulfil his material, or his intel-lectual, or his spiritual life. This is why we may say that each Church is the divine society taking flesh in a certain period, a certain social group, a certain area, in a well-defined section of life which it desires to christianize.

This incarnation is in fact a condition of its success: the distinctive missionary activity of the Church is to introduce the divine leaven into the dough of every human group. It is not her aim necessarily to mix up all the lumps of dough so that one solitary piece of leaven is enough. She does indeed tend to diminish whatever divides men and to increase all that unites them. She does indeed desire that there should be no impassable barriers of separation, but when she discovers such a barrier she simply crosses it, and on the other side creates another Christian group that will one day rejoin the first. This acceptance of reality on the Church's part has sometimes led to accusations of time-serving, but it is in fact a carrying out of Christ's will—that every human group should receive the leaven of the Gospels.

Having clarified this idea of the " mission " territorially, let us try to do the same on the cultural level.

A missionary must never Frenchify a Chinaman, he must not Europeanise him as a step towards converting him. His job rather is to build a Chinese Church—one hundred per cent divine, built on the Gospels of Christ and the doctrine of His Church: one hundred per cent human, incarnated in the country, its lawful customs, its race. For it is not individuals only that must be christianised, it is the society also, the institutions, the manners and customs. The impetus of missionaries has often been checked because they have not understood this. Proud of our western culture, we tend to make it for the natives a preliminary condition of faith.

We talk like this today a little glibly—we must remember that it could not be seen so clearly by a previous generation. Yet it is true that the Christianity they preached was too often not Christianity pure and simple, but rather a Christianity already wearing the flesh of, already incorporated in, a particular civilisation, *our* civilisation. It was a Christianity that, to be fully understood, fully lived, seemed to demand first a conversion to that civilisation.

An example of this in the material order may be seen in church architecture. Run over some missionary magazines and note how the same Gothic or Romanesque churches, cold and commonplace *like our own worst nineteenth-century products*, are to be found in Indo-China, the Congo, the Fiji islands. . . . Should we care to see the Temple of Angkor rising on the banks of the Seine instead of Notre Dame?

But today things are changing; it is one of the glories of that great Pope, Pius XI, to have launched native Christian communities, giving them leaders taken from among themselves. These native communities have now grown up, and for them there is no risk that Christianity should seem an imported article.

WHAT IS A MISSION?

The true missionary has gone forth to *create* a Church, not simply to enlarge the Christian community to which he belongs, not to make an annex to it, like a European firm establishing branches in the colonies. The true missionary goes to offer the Good News of Christ to souls which—justified, enlightened, sanctified, guided by the Holy Spirit—will create with his aid and to his admiration a new incarnation of Truth in a new human society.

THE word " milieu " really means middle or average. Men live in groups, in more or less narrow communities, and man is so constructed that the average way of thinking of the greater number of those among whom he lives tends to impose itself on him—not as an absolute imperative but by a continual invisible pressure, ending always (to a greater or less degree according as his character is strong or weak) in making the individual resemble the group he lives in.

Hence these social groups, these communities, have themselves come to be spoken of as milieux. They are made up of masses and leaders: but note that the leaders, though they influence the behaviour of their milieu in certain respects, are subject to it themselves in many others. This is in fact a necessary condition for their membership of the group and thus for their being able to act upon it from within.

Schools of sociology take note of four elements that go to make the social group what it is. First a certain geographical unity, although this is greatly diminished by modern progress in methods of transmitting ideas; the second—and in the case of the workers the determining element—is the organisation and the nature of their work; the third is a common conception of life; and the fourth the customs, habits and laws that go to make up their way of life.

Thus each individual belongs simultaneously to several milieux if his life is at all varied—for instance to the milieu of his work, of his neighbourhood, of his chosen amusements. And in some respects these environments overlap. X, for instance, working at the Renault factory—a very marked environment, with its hybrid brutalising work—belongs also to the wider environment of the workers of Paris, and again to the widest environment of all—that of the working class as a whole. Each one of these milieux has its share in the profound effect made on the man by his life as a social being, the inner circles affecting him most by their manners and customs, the outer by their institutions—school, radio, the Press and the like.

In speaking of a proletarian milieu we are using the word in its widest sense. Observe that this milieu is something negative. It is made up of an assemblage of smaller milieux, all characterised by their emptiness—lacking heritage, lacking culture. Can a sheer negation become matter for an incarnation? No, it must be destroyed.

Yet beneath the negation exists a mass of very real milieux, true subjects for an incarnation, possessing often hidden elements of richness and beauty which in an ordered synthesis could become a culture. Here are the workers in a certain factory, a group of campers, the families of a particular district, the printers who are part of a corporate organisation, etc. All these together, joined with many more, go to make up the popular environment; and contemporary sociology proves the influence the environment has on the individual. Even strong personalities are sixty to eighty per cent the result of environment, about twenty to forty per cent representing their personal contribution. Feeble personalities—the masses—are ninety to ninety-nine per cent their environment. And it may be noted that the great evil of our urban life is that basically-rooted social groups have ceased to exist, hence feeble characters simply drift.

These basic groups must be re-constituted.

Hence the choice for a Christian conquest must be between winning over the *real* milieux that are to be met with naturally and a conquest by artificial means: taking Christians out of their natural environment to place them in another.

While both these means are lawful and both have been employed in the Church at different times, it appears to us that by the first only can the world be made Christian in our present age.

We hope all these definitions and precisions will be forgiven us—it seems necessary to underline the state of the problem because of the existing indefiniteness which in the end changes the meaning of words so that we fail to understand one another at all.

WE must now describe a little more closely the areas we have called missionary—areas in which the institutions are pagan, the moral atmosphere is pagan, the people individually are pagans, and the natural law itself has become so diminished that consciences react to it only irregularly and incompletely.

Here we find no trace of Christian traditions: for even if some of the inhabitants have come from Christian areas, their traditions have stayed behind in Brittany or in Auvergne. Traditions are only transported if the people are moved in definite groups which continue as a community within the new community into which they have emigrated. As long, therefore, as the generation lasts which was Christian in Brittany, Auvergne, Arras or Mazamet, one cannot qualify the area as wholly pagan; the milieu is pagan, the individuals not completely. But by the second generation not much of the past remains, and it may be said truly that the third generation is utterly pagan. The gradualness of the falling away serves to explain the strange fact that so many priests are hardly conscious of the disaster: appearances deceive them. At the time of the war of 1914 the generation of the forty-year-olds still kept many traces of Christianity—they gave proof of it on the field of battle. But the eighteen-year-olds were much further away, while those born after 1919 for the most part make up the pagan proletariat we are discussing. What will happen to the generation now growing up unless we succeed in winning them?

It is not hard to define the nature of this paganism: we have met it too often. It has been well described by M. l'Abbé. Thus, in his study *Mission du Clergé*, as a disaster which is less the fault of individuals than of a tendency dating from the Renaissance and the Reformation and now beginning to show

79

all its hateful results. This is the tendency to separate religion from life.

"When," says M. Thus, "you question those who are in parish work, you are struck by the similarity of their answers. The last half-century has shown immense personal effort, both in the search for new techniques and in the deep potential of apostolic action. . . . Yet on the whole these priests have an impression that much of their work is vain, as though powerful and persistent energies permanently thwarted the fruitfulness of their activities. Sooner or later they utter the word 'atmosphere'."

A country is pagan where a pagan atmosphere has triumphed over the old Christian culture. Many of the Andrés, Georges, Jeannettes we shall instance are to be found no doubt in a Christian country, but there, as we have seen, they are themselves Christians who know when they are sinning. They are Christian sinners: sometimes they fight, often they repent, always they know what they are doing. But here they are pagans, not knowing good from evil, following the stream, itself pagan, that is carrying them away.

André is invited to a wedding; after the day's rejoicings he goes to bed in an adjoining room—and naturally a girl from the wedding party goes with him . . . and everybody thinks it perfectly normal.

Jeannette is engaged and her young man asks too much of her. In the end she gives in, and says unrepentantly, " I regret nothing. That's what love means."

Eugenics—even in its most evil forms—does not shock our Parisians. Whenever we have explained its theories, whether in meetings of girls or young men, someone was bound to remark, " Well, that's a very good idea "—and there was a chorus of agreement.

Even mothers' meetings in the Arrondissement furnish deeply interesting matter for study. How does the refrain go— " My little boy is so well, so big, so handsome." A mother weeping for the child she has lost cries, " He was so handsome, so happy," and the father adds, "He'd already cost us a lot of money."

The horizon of such parents is a narrow one. But, in fact, the public opinion of working-women above thirty is that a man who in the world of today gives his wife a child is either a bungler or a fool: in fact an absolute imbecile. You should see the indignation caused by such news, indignation that is certainly not feigned. To call a child into existence is by many thought of as irresponsible and unjust. "If you don't care yourself, at least think of him."

An entire absence of maternal instinct in women over thirty is almost universal among the really pagan proletariat. And, commonly enough, it is felt that a man has a right to "enjoy himself", and that a woman's one concern is to do everything that helps to keep him.

In one place, in an office of forty women, seventeen, in a period of eight months, had abortions which stopped their working. It is almost a dogma for these women to let a husband do what he likes and get out of the results as best they may. So high a proportion of abortions seems the mark of an exceptionally pagan milieu, which has grown up since the war; but the mentality of those women who will do *anything* to keep their husbands, and even view it as a duty, is common enough in pagan areas.

At one meeting of young married women, *all* present admitted to their *directrice* that their working companions had asked them if their husbands went in for perversion with them. On their answering no, they were laughed at and assured that their husbands were either poor creatures or went elsewhere for their pleasures, "for men can't do without".

Abortions do not occur just as an occasional sin of weakness: they are so common in Paris they equal the regular births. True enough, abortion is practised also in areas where the Christian outlook persists, but there it is recognised as a crime and kept hidden; among the proletariat abortion is perfectly open. Young Christian girl workers have told us, for instance, that women who have procured abortions explain what happened when they return to work—" and everybody quite understands."

A custom on the increase is for her fellow-workers in a shop or office to club together to give a girl for her wedding everything she needs for an abortion just in case she " gets caught ": all done up in a pretty little box with directions for use.

Nor is it concealed in family life: how often have horrified girl militants come to tell me, " My sister just had an abortion," or even big boys who realised perfectly that their mother had done the same thing.

Immoral attempts on little girls by their fathers, brothers-in-law, brothers and neighbours are far more common than is usually supposed.

I remember a case of a young girl seduced by a boy who was boasting of it in the neighbourhood. She wanted him to keep quiet. Her associates, her fellow-workers, her family even, showed an utterly pagan reaction. " There's nothing to cry about "—" Is this your first adventure? "—" Don't be so dramatic about it "—" Your story is just everybody's."

Another revealing fact is that photography of a naked girl has become quite a regular thing—like a First Communion or wedding photo. The girl gives it to her fiancé and he keeps it in his note-case. This is absolutely normal, and peculiarly characteristic of a pagan milieu.

Another bad symptom is the dismaying increase of self-abuse among girls, especially in youth centres and even in schools whose curriculum is one of a wide human culture. Skilled observers have noted—and we ourselves have noted also—the same thing in women's convalescent homes. The average indeed is so high in some of these places that we should not dare to publish it, hoping that these particular homes, being chiefly frequented by Parisians, are different from the rest. The thing is regarded as normal: most startling of all is the observation, " Everyone does it, even Catholics. It can't be a mortal sin."

Again, what alarmed us most lately in a mining town of the south, where the work is excessively severe, was not that bestiality (in the modern sense of the word) was now so widespread among women—for, alas, such a fact has now nothing surprising in it—but rather the fact that the young Christian working women spoke of it as mildly sinful certainly but, after all, forgivable enough. "It does no harm to anybody." It is said that women are the final guardians of the morals of a community. Alas, in our urban proletariat, this last rampart is already badly crumbled.

The atmosphere of an institution arises in part from the spirit in which it was founded, still more if its appeal is a popular one, from the mentality of those who make use of it. This is why all the new institutions are in a popular urban area penetrated with paganism to such a point that one asks if some of them can ever be purged: the cinema, youth camps and hostels, and especially those "free holidays" in the country which appear more satisfactory but are, in fact, even more unhealthy.

Ours is a paganism that has reached the very heart of life, and it is in the foundations of their structures that our great populous towns are pagan. The rage for certain plays, films, novels of pagan outlook is hardly surprising: the moral of one highly successful picture was "Love justifies everything".

While writing this last page I have been interrupted three times. First came a young man who wanted to discuss his last objections before conversion. He is intelligent and straightforward. Here is his chief problem. The Church forbids intercourse between an engaged couple before marriage. But "if you love you've got to do it"; besides, "how can you commit yourself before knowing something about it?" He is perfectly honest, he is not seeking a justification for what he wants to do, he is genuinely trying to get at *the ideal*. But he is so greatly influenced by the pagan atmosphere that it is exceedingly hard to make him see he is mistaken.

Soon after him came in a girl, pretty and well turned out.

She is going around with three young men, has promised marriage to each, and is uncertain which to choose. Possibly I helped her in her selection, but I am not at all sure I succeeded in showing her how deceitfully she was behaving. She wanted to choose two of them, " because if I choose only one and he lets me down, I won't be able to get married at all ". Yet this girl is not without intelligence and even refinement. She is simply hopelessly frivolous, not by temperament, but from lack of cultivation of the affections, lack of solid doctrine.

My third visitor was a Catholic Action leader. At the last committee meeting, the chaplain being absent, during a discussion of the respect owed to one another by engaged couples, it was agreed by all that two fiancés who gave themselves wholly to one another before marriage, although sinning, were only sinning venially " because they are engaged ". So much are these young people affected by the surrounding atmosphere that they no longer have any sense of sin; and they lack knowledge of Christian teaching so elementary that it has never occurred to their chaplain that it could be necessary to impart it.

A Jocist, speaking to a French workman in a German war factory about his misconduct, tried to move him by the thought of his wife waiting for him at home. The man began to laugh and produced a letter from his wife that said, " Have a good time. I know men can't do without it—as long as you don't bring anything back." And how common was the contract made before their separation: " I am free, you are free, but no ' results ' for either of us." We have had nearly a dozen letters from Germany reporting similar incidents.

It may be imagined how difficult it is to strike a chord, above all among the young, on the subject of a fruitful marriage. How can we talk of the cradle as a centre of happiness so as to awaken—I will not say sympathy but even interest—when the whole pagan world is suggestive of nothing but divorce, life in furnished rooms, above all no children. . . . And in most populous cities the civic authorities estimate the number who simply set up housekeeping with no formalities at double those whose marriage is registered.

Take another sphere of conduct: if theft or cheating comes to light in a business firm or a workshop, the matter is very simply dealt with: the culprit is sent away, but no complaint is lodged. What would be the use? The possibility of theft is always tacitly recognised; but some thieves get caught and they are sent away. This is surely the triumph of a pagan notion of justice.

George stole some cloth from his firm and sold it for ten thousand francs on the black market. Being found out, he had to refund, but at the legal rate—that is to say, he had to give his boss four thousand francs. He really does not understand, and no one around him understands, that the six thousand francs he is keeping are dishonest gain.

In these pagan milieux a man is not really considered dishonest who " gets away with it " and amasses a huge fortune by doubtful means. He is only dishonest if the police begin to pry into his proceedings—a thing that rarely happens. Look at the black market—the grand-scale black market where people grow really rich. Aside from food profiteering, is it thought dishonest to make a profit of five hundred to one thousand per cent? Among smart, go-ahead young men only true Christians abstain from these practices, and even they need frequent teaching on the principles of morality if they are not to be carried away by the atmosphere. " After all, I pay what I'm asked for a thing . . . and I sell it for what they offer me."

One more story—of that Sunday when a suburb in the south-west of Paris was bombed, including the Bois de Boulogne and Longchamp racecourse. More than a hundred people were killed in these localities and the tragic deaths were witnessed by all the spectators—by some in most horrible detail. Yet the crowd demanded that the races should be run. Very few realised the barbarity of it. They took place amid all the usual feverish excitement. People even protested at the entrance gates because, the current having been cut, the totalisator was not working. Next morning the newspaper *Petit Parisien* deplored this misfortune which had partly spoilt the races. Meanwhile two hundred lay dead, and more than four hundred were still in agony beneath the débris. I am not discussing the question of whether the management had good reasons for letting the spectacle go on. I am not judging them. But I do judge the crowd which knew nothing of reasons, but insisted on races. How near we are to the " bread and circuses " —the *panem et circenses* of ancient Rome.

But indeed the whole reaction to death reveals most emphatically the depth to which paganism has penetrated. Death no longer produces an act of faith in the after-life. Perhaps among certain women, certain girls, there remains a vague questioning, but for the most part it is pushed aside and the distress of bereavement is just sheer despair. Looking at these pagans we understand St. Paul's words to his Christians: " Be not sorrowful even as others who have no hope."

To understand what it means to mourn without hope one must have been face to face with these utter pagans.

Meanwhile, amid the pagan milieu that encompasses us stands out a small arrogant élite. Nietzsche's philosophy has its followers, its partisans, its propagandists. The superman becomes king. Certain pagans feel that they have surpassed Christianity, they have received an elevation of will and a nobility of soul that make them great men without their needing to be Christians.

Two Worlds

THE commonest Christian attitude in face of this engulfing paganism is to draw aside, to cling closely to one another, to join together in separated, isolated communities as men might in forests infested by wild beasts or like poor foreigners lost in the midst of hostile country. Thus Christians have created for themselves Christian communities centring on their churches. These communities do not correspond with any community of workers: the territory, for instance, of St. Vincent de Paul at Clichy spreads over five or six districts each with its own mentality and way of living. The parish of Lilas includes the former village (now completely transformed) of l'Avenir and the new garden-city district with its surroundings. It is the same in suburban townships.

All these districts taken together make up the parish—but this Christian community does not belong to its surroundings, it lives apart. It gathers within it people from every part of the neighbourhood (some being better represented than others), but it creates another and a completely separate neighbourhood of its own.

Shut in upon itself, the great concern of the Christian community is to preserve its immunity and safeguard its existence. Catholic children frequent a Catholic school—they do not play in the streets where the other children are to be found.

Catholic boys go to their own clubs. They exercise in their own gymnasium, they play football and basketball with one another, but they know nothing of the other boys with whom they ride daily on the Metro. But if they do not know their next-door neighbours they are well acquainted with all the working families of the parochial milieu, going with them to the parochial cinema, the parochial festivities, always meeting the same people.

Above all, they live in the same streets, buy from the same stores, those of good Catholics like themselves, of whose customers they form one definite section. The separation is clearly marked. Here is a negative proof of it. Since the breakdown of communications, the outer suburbs of Paris witness on Sunday evening a swarm of cyclists returning from camping or from a day's outing. There are trailers and cycles for two; young couples may be seen, and groups of boys and girls, ten rows wide, stretching out of sight making for the gates, and this for several hours on end.

Watching this novel type of endless procession, I asked some fellow-priests: " Are there many Catholics in this crowd? " And they replied, " Oh, no—and they would be horribly out of place there."

There still remains the world of work where all may be said to meet. For the young, however, this is not strictly true: many parishes succeed in placing their young people in Catholic firms where they quickly form social groups. In any event, mixing up in an office does not of itself make a community. People can work together all day long and have nothing in common: in a factory this would be more difficult: for there the common life is widened to include a measure of free time, which involves some degree of comradeship.

But it would be impossible to affirm that a community limited to working hours sets any profound stamp on the individuals who are subjected to its influence. And it is plain fact that a good Catholic, even if he likes his work, keeps up in his office, his factory, his shop, a defensive attitude which prevents him from mixing freely with his companions, which forbids him to become one of them.

What then is needed if Christians are to reach and to conquer the heart of this foreign pagan world—to which their attitude is far too often one of pure opposition?

What is needed is a small Christian community living in the milieu and radiating Christianity from its very midst. This the existing parishes do not provide.

Taking the parish of Saint Vincent de Paul at Clichy as an example, let us try to see the district and its community of Christians through the eyes of a " native " belonging to the pagan milieu.

" At Clichy," he would say, " there are campers who spend their free time in tents and have their club in the Boulevard Jean Jaurès. There are the swimmers with their locations in the Seine. There are swings for all the kids who swarm in the Place de la Mairie. And then there are the Catholics (only he would say, ' There are those who go to the priests '). There are more of them than of swimmers, but fewer than campers. They are quiet, rather soft, credulous people—old, usually, and eighty per cent women. They like to pass their spare time in the church—which is also in the Boulevard Jean Jaurès and is about as full as the Select Cinema, only it doesn't have a continuous programme. The priests live on funerals and endless collections for all sorts of objects, and the people allow the priests to exploit them."

Even if this is not very sensible, haven't we all heard it? Isn't it the common talk of our pagans? That they think like this is an important fact. Clearly the entire popular apostolate is hampered in going out for numbers by this problem of a parochial milieu, of a Christian community radically divided from the pagan community on which it should normally be acting.

An enlightening comparison might be drawn here with the mission field. When foreign missionaries have a European Christian community in their area, do they establish one parish or even one mission ? Or do they not prefer to work with a parish for the Europeans side by side with a mission for the natives?

These are two separate worlds which cannot be reached by identical means. The natives of the mission would be made uncomfortable by frequenting the European area, by being saddled with a whole civilisation they do not understand. Nor could European parochial Christians become very successful militants of Catholic Action among the natives. It would never be the action of like on like—and in our age this alone permits of deep penetration in new societies.

The clergy themselves cannot become specialised if they are teaching two such different worlds, cannot wholly adapt themselves. Their teaching is in danger of being indefinite, insufficiently " incarnated ", they cannot easily be at the disposal of both these groups.

Then, too, all missionaries recognise as a fact that the native community is not affected by the success or failure of the European parish—indeed seems to bear no proportion to it. The parish reaches its own milieu much more completely, but the mission is usually more vital and dynamic.

Does it sound paradoxical to say that this identical situation is met in our mission areas of France? On the one hand there is a Christian community of no vast enthusiasm, on the other a pagan world that could, if it were reached, bring forth young ardent Christians, revolutionised by the operation of the Holy Ghost.

Pagans and the Parish

A violent attack on the parish is with most people the result of a first realisation of the religious state of the proletariat. But an existent parish is what age-long institutions, an actual Christian community with all its historical and moral associations, have made it. Over this poor parish might well be hung a placard similar to that of the legendary pianist in an American theatre: " Do not shoot the pianist, he is doing his best." The parish, too, is doing its best. Actually what follows must be taken neither as a plea for it nor an attack upon it, but merely as an effort to find out the facts that make up truth. Truth is neither for nor against. Truth is.

The existing parish is then a Christian community. Its first charge is the perfecting of its members and it may also hope to widen its scope, to bring back the fallen-away, to win those who come near its orbit. The parish, too, may hope to cast its lines so as to catch a few fish in the proletarian world around it, usually remarkable individuals as human beings. When the parish has engulfed them their old world is left a little feebler, a little lower. To change the metaphor, its cream has been skimmed, it has lost some of its natural leaders, men who brought into it a little interest in morals, a little glimpse of the ideal. It has become more pagan.

Anyhow the parish is well aware that it cannot do everything: that the modern world has created, even in the professional order, needs that it cannot satisfy. It knows that the great cities with their changing populations, their weekly exodus, stretch far beyond its scope. Hence arise professional Christian unions—of Christian day-labourers, Christian postmen, Christian butchers, bakers, even opera-singers. These unions are framed in a parochial spirit: they aim at the practise of religious duties, prayer and mutual help among their members. Of course they exercise some degree of proselytism, and the parishes are glad to welcome them and work well with them.

The parish is, in fact, and rightly, rethinking and rejuvenating in this way its own apostolate and there is an immense work to be done in these fields. But they do not begin to affect the conversion of the proletariat, for the proletariat is simply absent.

The parish, even thus extended, hardly touches the pagan world: while still remaining the Christian community in a certain area, it must be further extended by a "mission." The missionaries may well be trained from among the existing Catholics of the parish, it will be a parochial charge to create means of perfecting the mission. But it must never be forgotten that the parochial organisation *by its very essence* lacks weapons against the surrounding paganism.

Philosophy teaches us that to act anywhere one must *be* there *aliquo modo* (after some fashion). In the proletarian world Christianity is present *nullo modo* (in no fashion). How then can the parish, that cell of Christianity, act where it does not exist?

In parishes known to us in popular areas sermons are preached several times a week clearly setting forth spiritual doctrine well adapted to a small group of enlightened and fervent Catholics, but the proletarian world around them remains untouched. Or again the month of Mary, of the Sacred Heart, of the Rosary, of St. Joseph, of the Holy Souls, are all kept, besides a weekly Holy Hour, Adoration on the First Friday, monthly and weekly Masses for various confraternities. All this works splendidly in building up a high type of Christian. Small, ardent groups of priests have given birth in the suburbs to fervent Catholic communities, but the pagan atmosphere of the area remains unchanged.

I have in mind especially two parishes, each in an area of about forty thousand inhabitants. The first has a larger staff of clergy, it is far more alive, far more active; both are in popular neighbourhoods, neither reaches the real proletariat. The first has a fervent community of some five thousand Christians, the second a less fervent one of about three thousand; as to the extra thirty-five thousand, their state is the same in either parish. Supposing the second in ten years' time by the efforts of its clergy became as good as the first, it would have achieved something fine. But still the agonising problem would remain—what of those thirty-five thousand souls?

How then is Christendom to expand? for it must somehow get into the pagan world and bring the light of Christ there. Christians must become the leaven in that world. But they are utterly separate from it, so what is the answer? Surely that we must change our outlook and seek out in the community Christians with a missionary vocation. We must equip them for this; we must send them, well prepared, into a world that is not their own world.

In most cases the parochial community as such, with the existing parochial organisations, cannot become missionary: first because of the difficulty, amounting to impossibility, for the pagans to enter the Christian parochial world; next because of the almost impossibility for the Christian community as such to enter the pagan world. We must discuss this two-fold impossibility.

Difficulties for the Elite of the Pagan World

In youth the chosen few are easy to get hold of, for they are looking for a *mystique*, for a cause that they can serve. But as a rule it does not enter their minds that the money-making affair which their neighbourhood church appears in their eyes to be could reach the stature of their dreams, could fulfil their aspirations. They seek elsewhere.

A boxing champion who had for two years been tormented by his aspirations told his story to a friend.

" Up to twenty I lived like other boys the typical proletarian life—work on the one hand, the slavery of the beast going from the stable to the yoke and back to the stable; and on the other hand the life of a boy who is looking for joy and a good time. The world revolted me—unjust, selfish, no possibility of happiness in it. I was deserted and deceived by pals I had thought of as brothers. I ran after girls. But it was a girl who brought my time of riotous living to an end.

" I got to know her, as I did many others, at a dance. For a whole year we kept on meeting, but our characters and our views of life differed completely. She was a Catholic and went to Mass every Sunday, and one day it all bust up. I was twenty. Sometimes she tried to make me accept her ideal. Honestly, I tried to look at it straight, but looking at a lot of pious old women was not likely to make me change my mind. I had my own ideas about it all. I didn't know any prayers. From time to time I would talk to God in my own way, but I had my doubts of the result of these talks. If God really existed, would He have time to be bothered with a working-class nobody like me? Then I let it all go. I said to myself: ' It's all a bad joke, a game played by the rich to put the poor to sleep, to make them submit and be resigned to be workmen and the slaves of big business and trusts '.

" Belief in God was obviously of use to somebody—it was useful to the rich men and the priests, not to anybody else. The others, the unlucky fellows who had to gain their living by the sweat of their brows, they were useful for dropping something in the collection, that was all they were wanted for. The bosses often called themselves Catholics and they made their workers sweat for twelve hours and more in beastly sur-roundings, unhealthy and immoral, at jobs which lowered a man's dignity, made him into a machine or worse. And if the man was a Catholic he was supposed to accept this and think it all quite right.

" The rich can always find the priest at home: they give him more money for his poor and to keep his church going than fifty workmen could give in a year. And when one of those swells got married the organ went full blast and all the candles were lit. And meanwhile a workman was being married in a side chapel with his two witnesses, a few friends, a priest saying everything in a whisper and an altar-boy you couldn't hear at all. They were afraid of upsetting the grand marriage going on next door.

" Just the same inequality, the same injustice for the dead. So God was for the rich, not for the poor. His sacraments were for sale. Of course He likes the rich man's offering better than the poor man's. No comparison. And yet the Church says, ' Men are all brothers. Love one another.'

" One day I went to see a priest. All this business had upset me; I wanted to know, I wanted to get it all out, to say what was in my mind. He was a swell guy. I often went back to him because he was understanding and I got a bit out of what he told me. Then one day I was roaming around the markets and I met a fellow who had a thing in his buttonhole like *she* used to wear. We picked up with one another. I liked him: his name was Marcel Fournier. He was out of work.

" ' You believe in God? '

" ' Yes, old fellow. How about you? '

" ' Yes . . . more or less. . . . Oh, you know . . . I'm not very well up about all that.'

" ' If you like I can help you to know Him. Come tonight, there's a meeting.'

" So I went, and I went again. After that I never missed a meeting and I found a wonderful pal: Christ the Worker, a good pal; you can talk to Him in bad times and good. I found that instead of God being impossible to get at, He was born in a stable—yes, a real stable. For thirty years He worked hard enough to get callouses on His hands. Thirty years of a life like mine. Thirty years of slavery, when workers hadn't a forty-hour week or paid holidays. And He turned the world upside down with twelve men He had chosen as His followers. And He set to work to explain His ideas, the Ideal He had come to bring to the workers of this world. Anyone who came near Him was won over by Him. He was a wonderful leader. And He was not afraid to talk to street girls so as to save them or to show the rich man who blamed Him for it where to get off. He said, ' Love one another. Help one another.'

" Now I was beginning to understand something about His teaching and what it led to—the solidarity of men. And He was a workman Himself, a carpenter, a fellow like me.

" Then what about the old bigot who comes out of church between two prayers to abuse her neighbour? She's humbug. And the so-called Catholic employer who thinks more of his machines than of his men? He's phoney. And all those people who come to church and whose life is nothing but selfishness, unkindness, injustice? They're just ersatz Christians.

" He got too powerful, that workman; the people were won by Him; crowds followed Him. The thing had to be stopped. So they took Him prisoner, called Him a ' seducer ', condemned Him to death, killed Him. But His work is still there. He said all that was needed to start a new world. There are others who have followed Him, are carrying His torch and fighting His fight all the time. I feel proud to be with Him and do my bit, because I understand now that you don't pay for the Sacraments but only for a bit of outward splendour. But I still don't understand why priests who have so much to do bother to become salesmen of outward splendour.

" I've learnt a lot at the J.O.C. and I am happy now, for I have an ideal I can take into the streets: to do good and work for a better world as He wants me to. For He is my strength and my joy."

Is this a solitary history? And do they all end equally well?

Difficulties for the Ordinary Working-man

In the actual state of things conversion presents for the ordinary worker difficulties comparable with those experienced by a pagan in a foreign mission. He has not only to leave the evil things in his life—he has to leave his life as a whole: his friends, his relatives, his customs, his Sunday outings; he must change his manner of life. He has been living in a proletarian world; he must leave his world.

To ask this of him is to ask for heroism—to a degree that we cannot imagine. Small wonder that many hesitate, that some recoil.

They are leaving what they know, leaving what has made them; and, as they look at it, our parochial world seems to them timorous and shrunken, terribly *bien pensant*, terribly old-maidish. It seems to them (I have heard this so often, false though it is, that I hope I may be excused for setting it down here), it seems that to love Christ they must accept a lowering, a lessening of their personalities. They are men, tough men, workers. They hate the " inferiority complex " of the " pious " Christian.

Nor is this all. What makes the difficulty greater is that what Christ wants is not only individuals—He wants numbers. And here we face not merely a difficulty, but an actual impossibility. For the average man in any community does not live alone; he will never abandon his milieu unless others go with him. Indeed he will never abandon it at all; he is not the man to run the risk of losing his place in his own society with all its consequences. Even with the young this is true, although in differing degrees. For adults, for family groups, it is a sociological rule—with very occasional exceptions, but with the same sort of overall verification as a law of physics or biology.

But here the reader may well be asking: Why postulate as a necessity that the converted proletarian must abandon his milieu?

The answer is that the parish and the proletarian worlds are not merely separated, they are also utterly different. Parochial Christianity, reconstituted in France during the birth of the middle classes, possesses its own culture: Catholic, of course, but soaked through with a bourgeois mentality, coloured by bourgeois qualities and by bourgeois defects. A great preoccupation with what is "respectable", a concern with refinement in appearance and in speech, a sense of order, good administration, well-run accounts, a certain good taste. All these smaller virtues, useful in finding a place in life and starting a family, are apt to look pale and ungenerous when transferred into the Christian and apostolic field.

And in practice these lesser virtues often enough issue in an individualism which shirks community effort—which, for instance, rejects liturgical prayer because it calls for the participation of all, which feels repugnance against becoming a militant in a movement organised for Christian conquest.

Then, too, for the proletarian the whole exterior side of worship presents its difficulties—the class distinctions in marriage ceremonies and funeral processions, hired altar-boys, payment for chairs, the opening and shutting of churches, the material externals; the very services that should draw him to the church and keep him in it have ceased for him to be common prayer; he does not understand them at all.

I remember a solemn All Saints' Day in a surburban parish. There were Vespers of the feast, Vespers of the dead, recitation of the Rosary, Benediction of the Blessed Sacrament. It lasted for two hours, and not one word was in French except the Rosary. A professional choir sang to an " audience " of some three hundred—and that number was considered remarkable as being much higher than usual. The clergy were in their stalls, the altar blazed with electric light. This parish had in its care more than fifty-five thousand souls. In the streets an animated crowd milled back and forth full of vitality, long queues outside every cinema. Three hundred in the church; the rest outside; the contrast moved me to tears.

Try then to imagine our proletarian coming into a parochial milieu. Too often we treat him rather as a missionary would who chose to begin by teaching a pagan French, putting him into a European dress, teaching him our manners and customs, when he should be teaching him the Gospel.

Of course it is easier to teach Christ's religion in an existing context. But the question must be asked: Why first convert to a culture and make acceptance of that culture a condition of acceptance of the faith? We are astonished when our pagans hesitate or refuse to come to church. But are we facing the problem in the right way? Should not a Church be founded in their midst? Should not they create and then live in a Christian community, a Church? Some of our mistakes may arise from our forgetting the true sense of belonging locally to the Church.

In any case let us face the fact courageously: in mid-twentieth century the faith is not preached in one whole world; millions of Frenchmen have not the Gospel preached to them.

Difficulties of the Parish in Penetrating into the Pagan World

If so many difficulties prevent the pagan from entering the world of the Catholic parish, cannot our Catholics go to the rescue? Theirs is the office of light in the darkness, of leaven in the dough.

Yes, a small picked group will hear this call from Our Lord, will want to be missionaries. *And then they must leave their own world to take the faith into the pagan world.* Can we desire that this noble office should be the business of all Catholics? Workers are needed first to rejuvenate the world of the parish, to imbue it with a deeper and more vital Christianity. And then is it so easy to leave one's own world to become a missionary?

Mademoiselle Jeannine, daughter of good parents, wants to become a factory worker so as to be a missionary to her proletarian sisters. (This has happened among Jocists, both boys and girls.) Is it to be imagined that she can do this and still remain in the pious world of Clichy Catholics? No; if she is indeed to be the leaven in the dough she must become, in everything except sin, an ordinary girl of the Bac d'Asnières district. Christ became man like ourselves in all things except sin, and our missionaries must adapt themselves to the ways and manners of the pagan peoples they are evangelising.

How, for example, are these pagans really helped to keep or regain their purity by seeing that girls of good family in a Christian world are pure. " If they were in our place, they'd soon see." And, indeed, of all Christianity as practised by the bourgeoisie, they are apt to say with a touch of irony, " That's all right for ' good girls '; there's nothing in it for us."

Mademoiselle Jeannine must give up the externals of her human culture, her refinement, her speech, her associates; she must follow her new companions into their world, speak their language, mix in their society (when such mixing is innocent), go out with them. Apart from all this there is no way of showing Christ to them.

Should this abnegation be asked as a general rule? Think of the conditions of life in some of the really proletarian blocks; drunken men who beat their wives, family scenes, shouting and yelling half the night, the promiscuity in the courtyards (van der Meersch's novels are not the least exaggerated)—ought a young Christian couple starting their married life to be asked to go and live in these quarters? Not all work-men's dwellings are of course so bad, but close and continuous contact with pagans, real pagans, even if they have a veneer of civilisation, must necessarily be painful to good Christians.

Not only is it a question of whether we can demand it; have we even a right to permit it? Ought we to send our young or even our older Catholics among the mixed hordes of a popular quarter? Those long accustomed to it find no great danger, apart from a certain lessening of sensitivity in the externals of modesty, but for boys brought up in other surroundings it spells catastrophe. Of this we have many examples.

Which among our Catholic families would be willing to send their boys to penetrate into the heart of a band of wild hooligans? Yet such the street-boys of these quarters commonly are. In one place the chaplain of the Jocists did send them to spend their free time mixing in really proletarian groups, only to be attacked furiously by the Catholic parents. "We send our children to you to have our minds at ease about their education, and you send them among dirty young blackguards in the streets." The poor man! His rector agreed with the parents and reproached him with some energy. Nor could they be reasonably expected to act differently.

It would not be possible to send the good boys and girls of a parish into the youth hostels for both sexes which are, bit by bit, becoming a State institution. For a thousand excellent reasons, our episcopate in the south has taken a very grave view of the real dangers encountered there, both of actual moral lapses and of the growth of a false moral outlook.

Yet it is certain that in a few years these hostels will in one way or another affect about half of the working youth of our country. The great wave of outdoor holidays already so manifest in other countries cannot be avoided and is in itself better than the stupefying amusements of the city.

Besides hostels, we have camping. And all this, taken to-gether, makes up a world not without its dangers (against which the best elements in it are accustomed to contend);

but it brings together a largish number of decent boys and pure girls. Is this world to be left unleavened by Christianity? Has Christ abandoned these young folk because they are caught up in the doubtful institutions of their era? Yet where is the leaven to come from unless from Christians who have gone forth from their own Christian society? The weak will not stand firm. A real missionary vocation is needed, a true call from God, if Christians (even seriously prepared) are to be sent into the midst of paganism.

Propaganda by books runs into the same problems: it has been discovered that what brings a pagan to Christ may do actual harm to the young Catholics of a parish. Take, for one example, pamphlets of initiation into " the facts of life "; for pagans they are indispensable, if the foundation is to be laid of a true Christian conception of love—a conception they are well able to receive, as priests recognise who have worked in their world. Yet these pamphlets do harm to young Catholics who ought to be told the facts by their parents in a family atmosphere, gradually and in proportion as their needs arise.

If both groups are not suited by the same books, how much less can they be taught and moulded in one assembly?

Adults can undertake missionary activity more easily than the young—but it must never be forgotten that youth is the formative period. The man is set and rigid: it is very hard to change a man over thirty-five. True, a grown man runs less risk in his Catholic action—but the action itself risks the lack of edge. It may not bite in, it may easily remain always the external action of a foreigner.

In short, it is far from easy for Catholics, with the best will in the world, to make their way into the pagan world. Only a very few are called to this vocation.

Difficulty in Combining the Two Worlds

Supposing this pagan world were won over: would it be possible to combine the two Christian communities?

It would, but only *when both the one and the other are utterly Christian*. For Christianity brings with it a splendid human culture, but needs often for its perfecting several generations. Meanwhile. . . .

René is the leader of a bunch of jovial young fellows of twenty who come from afar off, and who in the enthusiasm of their conversion and their generous love speak with splendid ardour of Jesus Christ. They are surely true Christians like those of the early Church.

Yet when the good boys of St. Pierre's church club come back from a meeting with René's band they speak of Our Lord as " the big chief ". Their parish priest feels with truth that they have not acquired the immense zeal of the new converts, but only a fashion of talking and behaving which they affect the more ardently from their legitimately great admiration. Now they are neglecting the First Sunday procession—a thing which of course has no meaning for their new associates but which had been for them a useful act of devotion.

This is one example out of many. The converted proletarian is certain to retain the defects of his milieu—and not merely those of breeding.

Take another case. The Jocists, all-eager to win proletarians, and especially a " tough one ", bring him in, congratulate him loudly, make a fuss of him. He feels he has become interesting, he is the pride of the group. His cap is pushed yet more on one side, he spits a little further. But soon they get tired of him, and off he goes without having found what perhaps he was seeking: an Ideal lived by lads like himself.

A girl leader lately told her fellow Jocistes some stories of an unmarried mother converted in one area; of a prostitute, young in years yet old at her trade, in another. She added, " Try all of you to have successes of this sort, even if some of your friends give you up because of the company you are keeping." The " even " is symptomatic.

This leader was right in putting forth her appeal for missionary effort. Yet many priests will feel that into a Jociste section where there are girls, some only half-converted, others, although deeply fervent, yet marked with the scars of their past, it would be hardly wise to introduce steady parish girls who come from a club conducted by nuns. And this will be the view of their parents as well as of their pastors.

Such instances can be multiplied. Here is another typical case. A section of Jocistes realised they had lost contact with a whole mass of the working population. An alarming number of girls were falling into sin. The Jocistes decided on missionary activity: they would go to their sisters' help, would go out into the streets, would wait at the entrance to the Metro. Poor foolish little things. Their very ignorance of danger showed how remote they were from such a world.

By God's mercy no harm came of it; on the contrary (and this is not unusual), there was a " miraculous draught of fishes ". Many of these fallen girls (some had only sinned once in response to a man's craving) seemed transported with ardour for Our Lord when they were told that He still loved them, that they could rise again with a new life.

But, alas, what was to be done with this flock—among which were even some possible saints? They wanted to bring others in. They wanted (and for them there was no great danger) to go and tell the rest what had been told to them. It would be quite easy with only one convert, but now there were fifteen, with the danger of thirty tomorrow and sixty the day after. How could the thing be handled? They were genuine converts, ready to make every effort, but of course they could not be transformed in a week. There would be relapses, jealousies.

We beg all those who see easy solutions for life's problems to contemplate the difficulties in a case like this.

What actually happened was that out of the crowd two emerged who were able to make an immediate recovery, who could be assimilated in parochial life. Some good people were scandalised, but the two were kept and turned into wonderful Christians. But all the rest, having for an instant glimpsed their Saviour and cried out to Him, will fall lower than before. Because now they know—they know that even compassionate girls, disciples of Christ, can do nothing for them.

This instance is, I know, taken from a level too low to apply commonly. But for work-girls in any factory the difficulties, harder to describe because involving so many imponderables, are just as great. I will try with an imaginary situation to make the actual impossibilities a little clearer.

Three priests get together and go out to found a new Christian group in a proletarian area. They preach the Gospel and the doctrines of the Church—and the " natives " discover Christ's love and are overwhelmed by it. That is all the missionaries begin by asking. They leave them to their consciences, still uninstructed but generous and worked upon by the Holy Ghost.

There are in the area bands of boys and girls who have learnt that they must be good comrades—but it is not to be supposed that they have yet been able to grasp that it is asked of them never to have sexual intercourse again.

There is a group of men who in the full fervour of their beginning have decided to promote the coming of God's kingdom with all the energy of their souls—and, if necessary, with their fists. (Just try to teach them different!)

As for the women, their speech is of an appalling crudity. And all this is just the proletariat, not a lower level of baser elements, just merely the people.

What religious society could gather in recruits of this kind? The scouts, the parish clubs, the Children of Mary? And if a local group did try to handle them, what federation would take them on—without imposing tests that would discourage and disgust them? We ourselves have tried the thing, we have seen it fail, under far more favourable conditions.

Here is another instance from life. A youth from a pagan milieu, moved by God's grace, sees His light and enthusiastically carries the good news to his friends. He is young and dynamic, a born leader. A priest who understands the situation gives him every help and encouragement. He brings twenty of his friends into the parish, which is an openhearted, understanding one (if it were not they would not be received at all). The parish is proud to receive them and makes a report about it at the next congress. But it is dreadfully uncomfortable with them all the same. Their priest who loves them makes them understand the difficulties. Appealing to their good will he asks for one concession after another. And they, as their love for Christ grows greater, yield more and more—but they do not understand *why*. After a year or two the less malleable elements have drifted away. The rest are almost assimilated, but *they are not really in their own world*. They are a group apart. The club opened its doors to receive them—but *it has shut its doors again*. There are ten more good Christians and that is a splendid thing, but the pagan world is left worse off.

We have called the ten good Christians a splendid result, and so it is. Ten won over *en bloc* represents a rare success, a masterstroke. For what usually happens? The priest who helped them and who loved them goes away. The boys get married and no one looks after them. In their eyes " the curés " are very " bourgeois " and the parish is a dull old hole. That young priest, energetic, dynamic, youthful, made up for everything else. He goes away, their energies die down and (apart from a few exceptional characters) they are not incorporated into the Christian community. A great flame had seized them in youth: for two or three years they had been saints of a kind—and then they went back to their old ways in their old world.

This case is taken from the world in which assimilation is easiest—the world of youth. Boys (and even more girls) still have a certain independence in face of their society: they are more adaptable. With adults, especially with families, a really missionary activity can get them *as far* as these boys. The young are more malleable, more understanding. They will even take the first step, while grown people, especially married couples, wait to be approached. They expect us to adapt ourselves to their understanding and they will never recognise Christ's religion unless it is incarnated in their own world.

One especial difficulty has been remarked about the adult apostolate. In certain proletarian quarters about one fourth of the marriages are re-marriages of divorcees. They have founded a second family, a happy one perhaps; they are educating their children decently. " Converted " themselves, burning with zeal, these people want to go out and convert others. But they are not yet ready for the heroic act of breaking up this second home with no hope of reconstituting the first, for the true partner is often re-married also. Perhaps this heroism will never be attained; perhaps later on, they feel, things may settle themselves. But in the meantime, how is a parish—whose office it is to protect its members from every scandal—to accept as quasimilitants people whom they are driven by all their traditions to throw out as impossible?

It is not merely anarchists, or fallen girls, or professional boxers who cannot be integrated into a parochial community. It is the people of Paris as a whole—educated as they have been with no trace of Christianity. It is the fashionable dressmakers. It is Renault's foreman. It is M. Dupuy living most respectably in his childless home, which is very elegant and the type of an honourable pagan establishment. It is the artisan who has saved up a little money and acquired a little culture but has once and for all " judged the Church ", as he will tell you, and has found her wanting and will not go back upon his judgment. It is the engineer who has just come in to mend my telephone and who had enough curiosity to talk to me for a little while, but who feels infinitely remote from the Christian community of the neighbourhood. It is almost every man we knew in our regiment—and in the regiments of many of our fellow-priests—who will never become Christians by joining a group that they cannot help looking on as a world apart. It is, let me repeat, the whole of the working class, both in its extreme elements—from which especially we chose some instances because they are particularly revealing—and in its whole central mass.

Let us be realists, let us set down our statistics truthfully and we shall see that these sad remarks are the result of sad experiences which we are not alone in having suffered. Must we not even add that in the proletarian world any success that looks a little like a mass conversion does not last beyond the first generation?

The Heart of the Problem

We have now reached the very heart of the problem. We are in front of that brick wall against which we have, one after another during the last ten years, hurled ourselves in vain. We find a new road which seems to us promising—and behold at the end of it the wall is there again. Let us look at a recent instance.

Everyone has heard of Father Lhande and his grand and noble campaign in the Paris suburbs, of the enthusiasm it aroused, the splendid devotion expended, the vocations to which it gave birth. (Among these was one of the writers of this book.) Superhuman efforts were made to bring Christianity to this mass of proletarians: a hundred churches built by " the Cardinal's Workshops ", new parishes, the blossoming of various good works. All France was applauding, all France was full of hope.

Let us sum up the results. From one point of view magnificent—for a single soul is worth a lifetime of work, and many hundreds of souls were converted. But as for penetrating the proletarian world, the effect was almost nil. A hundred new Christian communities were founded, but what did they accomplish? Out of the pagan world they gathered a few hundred Christians who had fallen into it or who had been afraid to practise their religion in it. A few dozen more or less hostile families were even won over from the pagan and brought into the parochial world. Good works were started which there, as elsewhere, skimmed the cream of human values among the young; succeeding in holding some few of them. And today have not these parishes really become close corporations just like all the rest?

Often founded and managed by saints, they are fervent sources of Christian life, but without much expansion. At first their zealous founders often went fishing in proletarian waters. Then the disciples they gained merged with the parish, the proletarian world was again left to its fate.

How painful, how impossible for us to depict here the drama of many priestly souls who had hoped for something else, had wholly devoted themselves. . . . Some still hope on, struggle on—and run against the old high wall. Most of them change their aim and begin to look for quality rather than quantity. Does not, they ask, the love of one fervent soul make up to Christ for many pagans? And they begin to work for an élite.

Clearly this is no solution of our problem.

In 1936 France was within an ace of Communism although there were only about two hundred thousand members actually affiliated with the party and about two million in the F.N.C. which is in political sympathy with them.

Grasp that the " masses " are an inert crowd which is pushed about by various forces and never puts up more than a passive resistance. These masses can be led anywhere by a small minority. And if we are prepared to pay the price we may well be able to take possession of some of those forces which today are moving our masses. But we must not deceive ourselves. Never will leaders from inside the parochial world be able to become the chosen few who can draw the masses after them. We must win the natural leaders of and in that world, those who set the pace for all.

The strength of the Communists in 1936 was that, although the party itself was small, perhaps indeed *because* the party itself was small, they had managed to launch a real movement (in the sense given in physics to the word movement) right through the people, a principle that drew with it the strongest vital forces in the people's own world.

As this study shows, we have not so far succeeded in winning the living elements of the populace, nay, even in showing that we regard this as our business. The religious élite in these pagan areas is made up of excellent Christians but of no great influence in their world.

Because we have not got the leaders we have not got the masses.

The Church and the Proletariat

Is then the proletariat accursed? These little ones, the humble, the poor—no one seems to want them. All of us are the rich—if not with money yet with the wealth of being respected, of having good connections (which, at a time of scarcity and restrictions, is worth even more than money), with the wealth, too, of culture and traditions. And we are only too much inclined to forget the poor who lack all these things.

Christ preferred the poor.

There is one fact in the Church's history which should lead us to reflect deeply. The Church's members have their share of human defects and Christ is ever watching to bring back His Spirit, whom Christians are for ever losing. Under the impulse of the Spirit they think much of the poor and the little ones and they found institutions to care for them. But after a very few generations, these institutions, these societies, are working for less destitute people—the change is often marked.

How many societies founded to help prisoners are now doing something quite different?

How many teaching orders that are today instructing well-to-do girls were founded to teach the children of the poor?

How many societies founded to work in public hospitals end by opening nursing homes or boarding houses?

A founder picks up little street-boys and his spiritual sons conduct professional schools of which the pupils do not come from the level of the populace.

An order is founded for the poor of the countryside; it goes into the cities and takes on other sorts of work.

Scouting is started for street-boys and is quickly turned into the preserve of the better-off.

We are setting all this down, without bitterness, but simply as illustrating a law that runs through all our human activities.

What follows? Are the little ones, the poor, the humble, the proletarians always to be sacrificed, in spite of Christ's preference for them?

Or must we not rather endlessly and tirelessly strive for a basic renewal in the evangelising of the people? Never must so vast a human world be left so ignorant and abandoned.

WHEN a missionary society plans to start a mission in a new country or new surroundings, the Superior does not attempt to make a blue-print of the work in advance.

The Gospel is to be brought to these pagans. The Good News must find its incarnation in their human actuality, but this demands first a deeply honest attempt to understand their world, followed by various approaches, many of them tentative.

The Superior points out the greatness of the work to be done, and makes his missionaries share his own confidence in ultimate success. He emphasises the immense opportunities that lie before them, he strengthens them with so profound an understanding of Christ's doctrine, that they will be able to adapt it to their new surroundings without losing any fragment of divine truth. Next he points out certain dangers common to all missions which they must avoid. Pagans must not be forced to become Europeans as a condition for becoming Christians; more must not be demanded of them than they are able to give; missionaries must be patient and ready, if necessary, to begin over and over again.

This sort of general advice is all that we hope to give under the heading *Towards a Solution*.

We are living in an age of planners, and readers of today, once they have been aroused by the unfolding of a problem, are anxious only to be able to sleep peacefully the next night. They want the clear, detailed outline of a logical solution, easy to grasp, so that they can feel, " Oh yes, I see there is a problem, but I have the right answer to hand."

Life is not like that . . . and surely it is not Our Lord's way either. He tells us to ask for our daily bread, not for three months' rations. If He gives us light enough to set out by, need we demand to have the whole road floodlit?

Such illumination this book cannot give: it could be simulated by various imaginative effects which we relinquish readily enough. We have struggled too long with the changing and profound realities of life to attempt to offer a five-year plan.

The Christian Possibilities of the Proletariat :
1 . The Appeal of Christ

The Christian possibilities of these pagans are greater than we conceive, if only the right methods can be found. There is no difficulty in awakening their enthusiasm; the difficulty lies first in finding the best road for them, and then in affiliating them with, or making them into, a Christian community.

The leaven of Christianity has not lost its power: it can stir the mechanics of today, it can ferment in their midst as powerfully as it did with the dockers of the port of Corinth two thousand years ago.

This is not mere theorising. Experience has shown us how hungry for God are the masses. Two, three, four or more times, sometimes over a period of years God calls these young proletarians in the depths of their souls. They are only asking to be won over—not merely a small élite, but the vast majority of the youth, while in maturity only the shock of a crisis is needed to bring them. In our present world, crises are frequent enough.

Here are some stories in illustration.

René, before his conversion, after dirtying his body and his soul, would throw himself on his knees at the foot of his bed. By way of Confiteor he would say over and over to himself, "What a —— you are "; he could not remember a prayer, but, trying to recall a phrase or two, would stretch his arms out as he knelt, in the shape of a cross.

Charles and Robert often wandered round the churches to see if people who prayed looked happy and peaceful. (This is not at all unusual.)

Lucien went up to an unknown priest and said, " The fellows in my neighbourhood discuss things a good deal and we would like to talk to someone like you. May we come and see you? "

Yvette hesitated at the last moment to " go all the way "— and came to ask a priest's advice! (It is more usual, however, for them to talk to a comrade known to be a Christian—or simply to observe that comrade's way of living.)

Bobby the boxer brought to one of the writers of this book as many boys and girls as the priest could handle. It was his lack of time and not lack of aspirants to instruction that terminated this campaign.

Here are some even more significant stories.

Stationed during the war in a big town in the midlands, one of us offered his services to re-establish a Jocist group in a suburb. On the appointed day he appeared and found four over-age altar-boys—sixteen, seventeen, perhaps even eighteen years old. They talked things over: but what on earth use were these boys—they hardly knew any youths in the neighbourhood, they were the only big boys in the group. Something could be tried to help them to " stick "—which might also aid some of the younger club boys in persevering. Even this would be an achievement, but *not the mission needed in the area*.

One evening, however, the priest, in his military uniform, passing through the working quarters of the town, met a group of about twenty boys (eighteen to twenty years old) and four or five girls. They got into conversation and went together into the corner café to have a drink. The priest told them that he was a priest and talked to them about the Young Christian Workers.

This was the beginning of a section. Soon there were thirty and forty at the meetings and then the most generous spirits formed a circle of militants. Of course the girls did not come to these meetings, but they were influenced and for them, too, something was beginning. It was a case of the youth of the neighbourhood being led by their most dynamic elements. It became "the thing" to be a Jocist, and those who refused to join were "mugs".

Christ became a living ideal for these young folk. Gradually, very gradually, He would penetrate the very depth of their souls. But if the priest who drew them in had been a curate in the parish, would he not have been obliged to leave these turbulent neophytes on the threshold for a long while for fear of the reactions of good practising Catholics? For it must be admitted that, side by side with a generosity akin to that of the primitive Christians, there are to be found in their minds rather terrifying concessions to the circumambient paganism. One day in a discussion on legalised brothels, one lad remarked: "They're an evil, of course. But for them I shouldn't have fallen as I have. But we are used to them and cannot do without them. We must suppress them for our children. For ourselves we must make them moral." It would be hard to guess what he meant by making them moral! But his observation was typical. The best of these boys had given up such practices months ago, but the masses will not be *completely* cured until the next generation.

How did the story of this section end? When parish life had become normal again, the presence of such very imperfect Christians was felt to be unendurable. They sensed this feeling and drifted away by twos and threes. Three of the leaders remained. One grew discouraged and took refuge in a purely individualist religion. The other two carried on with the seventeen- and eighteen-year-old altar boys and parted from their old comrades. The popular mission is dead. Only a parochial group remains.

Then there was that section we knew in Paris where a dozen militants gathered in a little room on the seventh floor of an apartment house. How many lads did they not drag up out of the dirt to renew and remake them?

"We are not a real Jocist section," they used to say, "we're just a group of friends." But they were real Christians, and to be a Christian is to believe in Christ and give yourself wholly to Him. They talked of Christ at their meetings as of a big brother; they talked of Him at their work; they talked of Him to the boys lounging at the corners and the girls walking the streets. . . . And Christ Himself took hold of the most generous among them; the Holy Spirit worked visibly in them.

But oh! how chaotic and disconcerting was their behaviour! All sympathisers (and *what* sympathisers!) they brought with them to Mass—for it was, they felt, a glorious pageant. All who had made their first Communion approached the altar realising that they were receiving Christ (the great Chief) and praying to Him with the simplicity of first communicants. But they did not hesitate in the hope of winning a comrade to drink a cup of coffee with him before Mass, " as long as I did it out of charity and not greediness ", they would say.

The room where they met was small, with a bed and two chairs, clothes hung along the wall in an orderly fashion. There was no electricity: for light an oil lamp was put on the floor— and never anywhere have I been so aware of the working of the Holy Ghost.

Ten or twelve great fellows, ages nineteen and twenty, sitting on the bed or on a board turned into a bench, boys ready to give all they had to Christ. When three or four hundred francs were needed for some good purpose there they were—one boy gave two hundred in a single gift.

The meeting began by a quarter of an hour's meditation on the work of the section. There followed a look at their own lives in which many pathetic and sadly human stories were told and which often ended with a splendid " catch ". Altogether a number of the most popular young men of the area (and indirectly a considerable number of girls) were getting to know Christ in an atmosphere of ardent self-oblation.

They did not certainly become saints all at once: they fell often, but they rose up with the gift to Our Lord of their whole selves in a perfect act of contrition and with many ardent resolutions.

They would take the girls they were giving up for a last walk (which did not always end in being quite the last) to clear things up with them, and some of the girls were converted.

One boy insisted on his right to come to the " leaders' show ", i.e., the committee meeting of the section. The others opposed his wish, but he held out. The president decided they had better go out of doors and think about the question for twenty minutes: so behold them out in the narrow street walking up and down, solicited by street girls at every step. Soon the leader comes to the window and whistles violently through his fingers and they all go back up the seven flights, C. still insisting in his claims; the president took a crucifix off the wall and laid it on the floor next to the oil lamp. " All right, keep up your pride in front of Him. Tell Him that you're too conceited to give in. Tell Him you insist on coming to the Committee."

The next moment this regular young tough begins to stammer, and asks forgiveness for his pride. The incident is closed.

Another time the three leaders, B., F. and D., were angry with one another—some question to do with their " fiancées ". Things were going badly. The President asked for fifteen minutes' meditation: it was heartrending to watch them with sombre faces in three corners of the ill-lighted little room. At the signal that time was up they rose and each turned towards the wall on his own side of the room: and each wrote on the wall, " B.F.D. ne font qu'un ". Above this a cross was drawn, around it a circle. Strange that three minds should thus have worked as one—the exactly similar inscriptions remained to prove it. Later on if they felt inclined to quarrel they would look at the writing on their walls.

A volume would be needed to gather all the " fioretti " that made one conscious of a true outpouring of the Spirit, and to tell of all the souls come from afar off that were uplifted by contact with this ardent Christian atmosphere.

But it was impossible to go on simply like this: the boys had at last to be integrated into the parish. For chaplain they were allotted a zealous priest but one who had always worked with the middle classes. He could find no empty room, so he suggested they should meet in the sacristy, in the Salle des Mariages, which was filled with impressive furniture.

One boy who had lice had a delicacy about bringing them onto the splendid chairs ; another who was a plumber was terrified by the sliding of his heavy boots on the polished floors. Not a single one came to these new meetings, they went on with their old ones. But their section now no longer counted as part of the Federation and it soon crumbled away. For some time the boys continued to attend Mass, some of them still love Our Lord, still pray to Him, but, accepted by no Catholic community, they live in a kind of vague Protestantism.

He of the lice, the owner of the room, was a simple boy, but with great depth. He spoke seldom, but what he said came from the bottom of his soul. He had been unlucky from childhood, but after he joined the Jocists he began to save, hoping to found a family. It looked as though a little happiness was coming his way. He confided his savings to his fiancée whom he loved with a great love—but she deceived him and spent his small fortune with another man.

It was a shattering blow. For a while he still went on seeing a priest. But he needed the companionship of his fellows, he was not strong enough to live alone as a Christian.

One night he wrote in his Retreat note-book: " Dear Lord, I can bear no more. I am coming to you." He turned on the gas before he went to sleep. They found him a week later, alone on his seventh floor.

A common but not commonplace story often turns up in various forms.

One day one of the writers came in at about eleven and found a young man who had been waiting since eight—a big fellow of twenty—who spoke thus: " Last week at a ball I was talking to my partner about love—as you usually do when you're dancing. She was a pretty little brunette, not too flirtatious, with a beautiful soul that you could see in her eyes. Well, she said to me:

" ' You know all this talk about love is a bit unreal. We shall be saying it to someone else in a quarter of an hour; it isn't real love. The only person who really loves us is Christ.'

" I don't know Christ, but when she said someone loved me, I felt good, because no one has ever loved me."

And the young man told the priest his sad story, the sort of story so often heard from these boys. He then continued:

" Well, I asked her for another dance to get to know who Christ is and why He loves me. She said:

" ' I explain so badly, but it's certainly true.' And she gave me your address so that I could come and get you to tell me all about it—and here I am."

The boy proved to be a good tool-maker from a well-known firm, full of common sense and a natural mystic. He did not yet know Christ, but they talked of Him together far into the night. The next morning the boy begged for Holy Communion and he became a fervent disciple, but they could not get him into the local J.O.C. which was made up of young parishioners.

" They're not my sort," the young convert explained. " They're nice little brats, but they don't understand me."

This was before the war, and the priest and convert wrote to one another while the war lasted, but during the débâcle the boy was lost sight of. What became of him? We hope that God called him to Himself when he was in such a good state.

But perhaps he stayed in the countryside. Did he find a Christian community able to take him to their heart? Did he find a priest able to understand his method of confessing— which was simply to recount his life since his last confession, telling the good and the bad alike? This boy, like that last, was not strong enough to *live* his Christianity without a Church.

If he found no Church he drifted back, it may be, to his old life—like so many others.

A big volume could be, perhaps one day will be, collected about the worship of Christ by the pagan proletariat which is looking for Him. Girls will have a place in it and adults, too. We have been talking here only of the boys because theirs is the most poignant story.

Engaged couples are easily won over, for human love fills them with a desire for the infinite which comes very close to a need for an ideal. Everything in their lives needs rebuilding. The stakes are so high, the treasure so great that they feel weak and cry out for help.

Their lives have to be re-thought in terms of home and family, and they would rather, at this idealistic moment, rebuild as Christians if a genuine Christianity were offered to them. Strange as it may seem at this moment in their lives, good is easier than evil. All this is true, too, of young married couples.

Grown people's conversion is much slower than that of the young, but they might come over in a body, as they do to Communism, from the need of an ideal. If in the doctrine of Christ they grasped an ideal—a truly working-man's ideal—they would give themselves up to it.

It is worth noting here that we are in fact living in a mystical period—within a generation the proletariat will most certainly have embraced some form of *mystique*. And we think, nay we are very sure, from all sorts of hints and signs, that, despite the black picture so often painted, Christianity can win a foremost place among the *mystiques* that have power to win over the rising generation.

But we must learn to offer it to them as did Saint Paul to the proletarians of his period.

All those who have been able to lay aside their own culture, who have given themselves totally to the people, bear witness that the catch is rich, is even miraculous. But what stops the apostle in his tracks is always the organising of a Christian community and its integration into the Church: so that we are tempted sometimes to cry out with Jeremiah, "The little ones have asked for bread and there was no man to give it to them."

The Christian Possibilities of the Proletariat :
2. Native Christians

Under this curious title I want to set down some stories of ideas and actions which appear to neophytes of the proletarian world to be the logical outcome of Christ's teaching.

A boxing champion had just become an ardent and militant Christian, determined to promote God's kingdom. It so happened that a young man of his own age, a "pal", living in the same boarding-house, married to a charming young woman and father of a new-born baby, was taking advantage of his wife's convalescence to misbehave with an unmarried girl. (All this happened not in a slum but in the normal working quarters of a large city.) The boxer tried to talk things over with his friend, who summarily dismissed and thereafter avoided him. Whereupon he evolved the following scheme: "I'll soon meet him in the passage leading to the Metro at Saint Lazare with that woman. I shall then insult him, put him to shame before her and finish him off with a knockout blow. He will feel so much ashamed that it will end the whole thing."

Off to a priest to lay the plan before him—rather to the poor man's embarrassment. Clearly it would be bad to let a family be broken up, but the means proposed fell outside the framework of moral theology, which only discusses *prudentes et benignae admonitiones* (prudent and mild admonitions).

The priest, however, after it had been explained to him that this was the only method, and a method perfectly natural for a boxer, gave his consent. He stipulated only that the reason for the chastisement should be explained quite clearly to all present, and that the results of the blow should not be lasting.

Believe me, the thing was done with the hand of a master. For a while the victim sulked—but the sinful connection was broken off, as prophesied. After about a month he suddenly invited the boxer to come for a drink and thanked him for what he had done. " You were quite right to take strong measures. I was making every kind of a fool of myself with that blasted little idiot who was always hanging round my neck."

The boxer got his friend's baby baptised and stood godfather. He had saved a family—and he continues from time to time to use his fists in the service of Christ.

Louis brought a friend to confession, a comrade of eighteen who had given up his religion immediately after his first Communion. He re-instructed him, and Edward the neophyte, overflowing with enthusiasm, began to long to be martyred or at least to have a tough time for Christ's sake.

(The scene of this story is on a social level rather lower than the last.)

Edward was living away from home. He had taken lodgings in a low-down boarding house at the end of a blind alley. The owner of the house was also a procurer, and while Edward was out of work he offered him a reduction in rent if he would help him in his special trade. (Edward added, with simplicity, that he had been used to pay himself in kind, but he had now decided to change his life and he bound himself to this with a promise.) That night he announced his resolution to his host, who laughed at him in front of everyone in the café. " You poor fool," he said; " you've let the priests get hold of you. I might lose my temper, but I'm a good fellow, so here's my offer. Come back tomorrow and meet all your lady-friends (here he added a few details). If you still stick to your word we'll never speak of the matter again."

Louis told me about it and I nearly hit the ceiling. " No, no, Edward must never keep that appointment."

But Louis explained that if Edward failed to turn up he would lose face. They would write him off as a poor fool, got at by the priests. And then the whole alley would continue to despise and reject Christ.

" Of course you could find him another boarding house, but not easily so cheap a one; besides, if Edward stands fast, a lot of men will get to respect Christ—perhaps even to respect priests—and perhaps some of them will come over. . . .

" I shall go with Edward," added Louis, thumping his hearty butcher's chest, " and you need not be the least afraid."

And so the alley witnessed a tiny gleam of Christianity—but there, as elsewhere, it seems to have no future.

Robert works in a huge ironwork and welding factory, near the Porte Saint Ouen. Since he has been a Jocist he has often made profession of his faith in Christ in front of all his comrades. One day an old man, who picks up a living from the gutters and pushes round a baby carriage on three wheels, found a fourth wheel for it; but the axle being too long, he came into the factory and begged of them the charity to fix it for him. The foreman asked Robert to do the job: he gave it brief attention and handed it back to the old man who still tried vainly to put on the wheel. Humbly and timidly he brought it back to Robert, begging his pardon for troubling him. Then Robert had a flash of light. That old man might be Christ: you should treat him as if he were Christ.

For twenty-five minutes he worked on the wheel, straightened the spokes, supplied a new pin, fitted it on to the cart, and then returned to his work. He went on working a while, but he was not happy.

He said to himself, " You did an act of charity for him, but you didn't love him. You treated him as a poor beggar. You didn't treat him as Christ." Robert suddenly saw what to do; he traversed the whole length of the building—a good hundred and twenty yards—went to the cloakroom, took out a packet of cigarettes from his coat pocket and began to run through the streets like a small boy in search of the old man.

He had already been round the neighbouring streets twice, overcoming his naturally immense human respect, when he found the poor wretch and offered him a cigarette, saying,

" Here, do take this. I fixed your wheel for you just now, but I didn't treat you like a brother. Shake hands on it."

As I tell this story I think of one of my fellow priests who complained that Robert's manners are bad. He may be right, but there are various kinds of good manners. Robert has a magnificent character. He became a foreman, giving the chaplain a good many headaches on his way up. His own view is that he refuses to be looked after like a little girl. But he certainly makes more demands on the chaplain's understanding than a parochial club boy.

Before he went to Germany, Robert decided that he wanted to visit his Cardinal—and in the interview he bore himself like a man. In his own world, his fashion of living, his Christianity is sometimes startling and disconcerting, but gives proof of a wholehearted generosity in which the workings of the Holy Spirit can be clearly recognised.

These stories have been chosen because, thanks chiefly to modern literature, the world of young men in a completely working milieu is the best known to our readers. Stories of the same sort, but less easy to convey in their full beauty, are to be found in the world of fashionable dressmaking, among the models and the saleswomen in the big shops of the Place Vendôme. Or again the naval and military chaplains and directors of various good works could all write volumes. Indeed many have written volumes—but they forget to tell us whether the souls they write of have persevered. It would be asking for a rare degree of honesty to press this question. Perhaps ten per cent? . . . And surely the good God knows what He is doing when He takes so many home to Himself. For as we meditate we recall so many, so very many, who died like saints, but who, from lack of a community, could not have lived as Christians in their own world: men, women, boys and girls. (Some among the poorest seemed to find something in the Salvation Army. The occasionally considerable success of this association with its vague beliefs is purely

the result of the crying need among Catholics which we are
lamenting.)

Some have sought all their lives what they have only found
when laid aside from active life—and they have died as saints.
There was Gina and Paulette, Julot (another boxer). There
was Léon and Paul and Sacha—and you, my dear Jean, who
wept at having to die alone in your hospital cell at St. Martin's
Sanatorium and offered your life of eighteen years for your
comrades in misfortune. . . . And so many others, worn out,
broken, grown old so young, to be found dying unknown and
not greatly loved in every hospital. . . . No, indeed, Our
Lord can never abandon the poor man. Too many saints are
praying for him in heaven.

A chaplain to young married couples told us that a sailor
may have a true love of God and yet hold out against sin only
in one port out of two. The thing has entered so deeply into
his way of life.

One curate told me that he made no further demand on some
newly-weds—whom he had instructed into a surprising degree
of preparedness for marriage—than the promise of a monthly
Mass to start with.

All modern observers are crying aloud that the man of our
times is sick, sick in his soul. To claim that he must *first* be
healed and *then* converted to Christianity seems to us at least
a semi-pelagian idea. The ordinary man, at any rate, can only
be made healthy by being made Christian, while, on the other
hand, only his return to health will enable Christianity to have
its full effect on him.

We have to accept as Christians humanly sick people, people
imperfect, therefore, both in their humanity and their Christianity. And this is even more true in our world than it would
be in many a so-called savage country where men have remained sane. Our external civilisation must not blind us to the
fact that we are decadents.

We must repeat, and repeat insistently: the Christianity of

our converts is often incomplete. It is very human, it is impregnated with the ardour of a human experiment, yet in it we may see clearly the action of the Holy Spirit. It is a Christianity of catechumens rather than of the faithful, a marvellous seed with promise of a grand harvest. But where, alas, is the ground for its sowing? We have splendid great fields under cultivation; what we lack are the frames and boxes for the seeds to germinate. And there are so many seeds waiting to germinate.

There are moments when one is tempted to cry: " No, my dear John; no, Robert; do not bring your friends who used to be Communists. We know they are looking for Our Lord, but what do you expect us to do with them? They simply don't belong, they have not our ways and manners, they are too remote from us and they will soon be conscious of it. Don't bring us that young woman from your factory, François—even though you say she would be a real Saint Paul if she were converted. Or at least only bring her if she can be converted all of a piece and become presentable in her very first conversation. No, don't bring us any more just yet; don't you see we are overwhelmed, we don't know what to do with them." For that immense crowd we need an organised catechumenate.

I REMEMBER it as if it were yesterday. In the midst of the rout of 1940 I met a priest on the road; and, possessed as I was by the agonising problem of how to make the pagan mass of workmen into Christians, I could do no other than talk to him about it.

He listened attentively, then began to laugh ironically. After a pause for reflection, he said:

" You people simply don't know what a mission is. Urundi-Ruanda in the Congo has about as many inhabitants as Paris (about three million). We have five hundred and fifty-eight thousand, eight hundred and thirty-eight baptised Christians and one hundred and fifty-six thousand and sixty-nine catechumens. According to what you say you have no more regular church-goers than we have—and our Christians are of a different kind. We have about one-tenth the number of your priests (one hundred and eighteen missionaries, forty-five native priests). Our pecuniary resources can't compare with those of the capital or of your great towns. . . . And yet Christ's kingdom is growing.

" And if we multiplied our priests by ten, if we had an impressive bank roll, if we employed your methods, our results would be the same as yours: the ground we had won would be maintained with difficulty; bit by bit we should retreat— *as you are doing*.

" Your methods are excellent, have stood the test of time, have been elaborated by generations of priests, very saintly priests, but they are suited only to a Christian country, to a rooted Christianity; they are the very antipodes of missionary methods. And you are seeking with these methods to convert a pagan country? "

He laughed again as if it were absurd to draw out the comparison. Then he grew serious:

"We receive as Christians only people who have had several months, in some more difficult missions several years, as catechumens. You go round imploring and beseeching families to let children make their first Communion of whom one in ten may persevere—and that is a high estimate.

"We baptise children only if we can be sure that they will receive a Christian education. You know we even oppose the baptism of native soldiers converted in France—for how are they to persevere if they have no Christian community ready to receive them on their return? You never consider this aspect of the question, yet it is of the highest importance.

"You baptise a child if he is a hereditary Catholic—for instance in hospitals and maternity homes. And why? Because you maintain the illusion that you are in a Christian community. But what the parents are saying is: 'Well, it won't hurt him. It may bring good luck.' Or perhaps, 'It will be a good thing later, when he comes to be married.'

"You try to marry everyone in church except divorced people.

"You bury everyone with a great following of clergy and splendid ceremonies, even if they happen to be divorcees or renegade priests, because in your parishes no enquiry can be made."

(When he asked me I was bound to admit that only one out of seven buried in our churches had received Extreme Unction, only one out of ten Viaticum—in other words, only one-tenth had received the Last Sacraments in a fully conscious state.)

The missionary concluded quietly:

"The great difference is this: you are assuming the existence of a Christian community which has in fact disappeared. You help crowds of people to perform acts designed to bring them to God individually. But nothing follows. You forget, too, that brilliant statistics are less important than the inner value of a Christian community. Thus you lose a great deal of time and employ many men with no appreciable result.

" What we do is establish Christian communities. We know the need men have for a society, however small, in which to live their religion. With us to convert, to baptise, is also to integrate in a Christian community, in a Church.

" Our task, which was re-emphasised for us by that great Pope of the missions, Pius XI, is to make hundred per cent native Christian communities, incarnated in the country, embraced in its atmosphere."

I have often thought over this conversation and read and re-read Pius XI's words, applying them to our urban mission field. Of course their application can only be analogical, the situations are not exactly the same; but still the analogy is most enlightening and helps us to discover remedies for our own ills, and to adapt methods to our own conditions. Two ideas, above all, should be enlarged upon:

(1) We must have fully native missions;

(2) Our religion must be religion pure and simple, stripped bare of all the human adjuncts, rich though these may be, which involve a different civilisation.

Fully Native Missions

The proletariat itself consists of a variety of worlds: all to a certain degree disinherited, all separated more widely from the world of the parish than are workers from bourgeois inside the parish. For culture, sociologists agree, divides men far more than social conditions, and the proletariat has no Christian culture. Missions would create one, but up to the present there is none. Not to recognise this fact is to want to make Chinamen practise Christianity with the external behaviour of parishioners of Saint Sulpice.

An example that is very typical may serve as a demonstration to those who are aware of the elements of the problem. The *Editions Familiales de France* have published a little masterpiece of a book by Abbé Bragade, called *Le Vrai Visage de l'Amour*, which poses the problems of love and answers them by telling the story of a young man preparing for marriage.

The scenes are set often around the piano, in the home life of good comfortable families, in the atmosphere of a parochial world possessed of a fair degree of culture.

Now imagine the same degree of Christian feeling, the same natural goodness, absolutely the same spirit fundamentally—yet could this novel be written concerning a world wholly proletarian? The language, the habits, the life would produce a story that simply could not be published.

In this case it is not a question of religion. I am supposing both worlds to be equally strict religiously: it is a case of two societies of which one is influenced by bourgeois culture and ways of living and the other not at all.

A fellow priest remarked to me that although refinement of speech and of behaviour are not Christianity, they do help you to be at home among Christians. Are we to conclude that their absence takes away the opportunity of belonging to Christ's religion and that we must wear gloves if we are to enter into the kingdom of the Father?

Pius XI's great idea, the idea which gave such a marvellous impulse to foreign missions, is precisely this: make the missions native in every possible way, native in everything that is not sinful.

In the Pope's mind this directive goes very far. First comes the formation of a native clergy. The Holy Father considers such a clergy as a primary condition of the apostolate. " You must," he writes in the Encyclical *Rerum Ecclesiae*, " work at it with all your strength, or else we shall judge that something is lacking in your apostolate—and even that you are delaying and slowing down the establishment and organisation of the Church in the area for which you are responsible.

" The clergy whom the apostles set over each new Christian society were not brought in from outside, but chosen and drawn from the local population."

Benedict XV had already said—and Pius XI quotes him:
"Naturally enough the native priest is marvellously prepared
to introduce the Faith among his compatriots, for he is united
to them by birth, outlook, tastes and feelings. He knows far
better than anyone else the methods of winning them, and he
will often be at home where a foreign priest could gain no
entry."

The Pope goes on to say that this is an indispensable condition for the permanence of a Christian society.

The argument for a native clergy does not apply in our case,
but *it is doubly valid as regards the militants of Catholic Action
who must be wholly representative of the world they are working
in.*

Native priests are not asked to forget their love for their own
world, their especial attachment to it; still less should we make
excessive demands on our lay militants.

"Their charity will be so great that they will be ready to
suffer, even to die for those of their own tribe and their own
nation."

Pius XI's thought in this matter goes so far as to make him
prefer new orders adapted to these new Christian societies to
the ancient religious orders conceived in the ancient Christian
world. Have we always a like width of vision and a like apostolic
courage?

As to the catechists, they should be chosen, whenever
possible, from among the natives and "their charge will be to
adapt the essence of dogma to the mentality and intelligence
of those to whom they have to offer it and explain it, in which
they will succeed best the more deeply and intimately they are
able to enter into the nature of the natives".

No, says the Pope, "to become a Christian must not mean
to abandon one's own world. New needs must be met by new
methods. Saint Gregory the Great advised Saint Augustine,
the apostle of England, not to destroy the pagan temples, but
to destroy the idols and replace them by the cross; not to
abolish the pagan feasts, but only the idolatrous worship; still

to celebrate the ancient banquets, but to transfer them to the feast days of the saints."

Even to dubious practices toleration is recommended if a sound interpretation can be placed upon them—as for instance in the case of the honour paid to Confucius when the civil authorities declared it was a national and not a religious demonstration.

The Apostolic Delegate to Japan told the missionaries to use the Japanese flag as a national emblem. " The influence of Christianity must win its way gradually over the pagan mind. And for its point of departure this influence must take the natural virtues of the Japanese people, to cultivate them, raise them up little by little, purify them of the definitely pagan elements with which they are still mingled." This, he added, was to be effected by a training at once Christian and Japanese. And he complained of too great an insistence that pagan pupils " who frequent Christian schools should be present at Mass and other acts of worship ".

And again, " In explaining Christian doctrine and the duties of a Christian, an effort must be made to destroy the common impression that to become a Christian means, even for a good-living pagan, a total change in his way of life and a break with Japanese traditions so complete that the Christian becomes a man apart, isolated from those who do not share his faith, separated even from his family and compelled to take part in observances incompatible with modern life."

The question is forced upon us: is not all this literally the fact with our French pagans? A convert from the slums of Clichy, a rough lad from Ménilmontant—surely they become " men apart ", isolated from their own world, separated from their families. Imagine them, militants of the J.O.C., obliged the first Sunday of the month to walk in a church procession, candle in hand, following a bevy of little girls and a lot of old women! Do not they feel themselves taking part in " observances incompatible with modern life "?

We might even be wiser not to insist too strongly at first

on attendance at Mass or other religious acts in the case of fallen-away Catholics who are gradually coming back, or of pagans whose period of instruction is not completed. Some of them are really only prowling around the Church learning to appreciate it: they have not yet come in.

Are we prepared to give them a training " at once Christian and proletarian "? Are we ready to recognise that the influence of Christianity can enter only *by slow degrees* into the mind of a populace deeply soaked in paganism?

Surely we are a thousand miles away in our thinking from this missionary outlook. Why then be surprised at our setbacks?

Nor have we the missionary outlook in our way of teaching doctrine. The Apostolic Delegate, quoted above, rejects " certain explanations of the catechism usually given which are not fitted to the Japanese mind. It is not a question of the doctrine itself, but of certain explanations that have been brought forward ".

We can gain light on our task from this remark also. Christ's doctrine does not frighten the poor, but only the way in which it is offered to them. Our Lord's demands they see as absolutely right. Indeed they are often carried away by them with intense enthusiasm. What puts them off and discourages them is our mass of little rules of human prudence, our cases of conscience elaborated in other epochs, suited to another age.

Pius XI, with true characteristic discernment and sympathy, warns us to avoid " painting with colours that outline the bad more than the good the habits, the religion . . .the way of life of pagan peoples, even if we do so with the intent of awakening a keener love for our brethren who lack Christ's light and of increasing the funds we are collecting for their assistance ".

This advice, too, we can apply to the case of our Parisian pagans. It is the accepted custom, when desiring to awaken the charity of the public or to obtain certain facilities for dealing with the proletariat, to insist in unmeasured language on their degradation, so much so that quite intelligent people are convinced that debauchery is the inevitable result of too small a workman's dwelling or that virtue is always in danger when a young man of the people goes for a walk with a girl.

There is quite enough that is pitiable among the pagan masses without the need of unjust generalisations or a naïve ignorance reasoning from pure theory. We have shown something of the true picture, but overall condemnations only add another solid difficulty to the task of the missionary who wants to found upon the natural virtues still existing in the proletariat a beautiful and all-embracing Christian faith.

By now perhaps we can see a little more clearly the qualities which his apostolate demands of the urban missionary.

The conquest of the proletariat is a heavy labour and may long be a barren one, so that all who undertake it must offer themselves in utter self-abandonment. This world of the poor is proverbially generous. Careless of the morrow to the highest degree, with a good deal of sound human nature at bottom, but much swayed by emotion, they demand also that their apostles should leave everything with no backward glance and no provision for the future.

And in return these missionaries—like those in foreign lands —have little reward to hope for. At the beginning of a Christian community souls rise splendidly but slowly, and even if the converts succeed in giving their world a shove forward, the first generation will not be very presentable.

Missionaries who become " of the people " (and how else can they penetrate among the people?) must be prepared to be a little suspect even in the eyes of their fellow priests. They have changed worlds. A task of this magnitude calls for priests completely ready to give themselves to this work beloved of Christ without much hope that they can ever take back the gift. There are departures for the mission field which offer no hope of return: perhaps these, too, are such.

These missionaries, too, can do no better than follow the directives of Pius XI.

First, not to create little Christian islands which bring them speedy consolation but where the solid work does not advance. The entire area must be transformed, even though this means slower progress. Listen to the Pope of the Missions: " You must have at heart the business of distributing your personnel so that no part of your territory is left without the preaching of the Gospel, no part reserved for later on."

Again in a missionary country you must not make commitments too quickly; you must not create " what may enslave you ". This, too, is Pius XI's advice: " Do not build at great expense splendid churches and other edifices. There is no point in preparing a cathedral and a Bishop's palace for a diocese that exists only in the future." (Here of course the cases vary a little. Suitable churches are needed in France to make people understand the splendour of religion. Yet there may be value in the warning as against construction in certain areas that make us *primarily* the builders of edifices " that may be ill adapted to the needs of a rapidly developing apostolate ".)

Finally we must not " institutionalise " too rapidly, for if we do we risk fossilisation. "Do not," the Pope continues, " allow buildings and institutions to draw you away from your missionary responsibilities. Too great an interest in them, too heavy a financial burden, must not tie down you or your assistants to the point where you cover your whole territory less and less frequently, or even where you omit entirely these most useful visits."

This sentence appears to us a summons to a missionary apostolate in the popular quarters of Paris. Are there not two hundred and fifty to three hundred thousand souls in areas where thirty or forty priests are exclusively occupied by institutions or by the service of little islands of Christians which, taken together, amount to no more than ten thousand faithful?

Religion Pure and Simple

To build up a fully Christian community in the world of the people is a work not without difficulties. But there is a second and harder job which it is difficult even to convey to the reader. In conversations on the subject I find I have been understood up to this point—and then my interlocutor parts company with me. A few unvarnished tales will best suggest the nature of the problem.

Jean was an anarchist: on his chest were tattooed the words, "No God, no boss". He was wounded during the Clichy riots of 1937, where he did some shooting himself. Jean was converted—without difficulty, for he has a generous nature in need of an ideal. Christ fulfilled that need, Christ became his ideal, the divine Personality of our Saviour carried him off his feet. I prepared him for his first Communion; he read the Gospel; chosen passages from St. Paul were explained to him. He was all but ready when I was called away. A nun undertook to finish the instructions, but on my return I found everything broken off. I couldn't understand it. Jean was heroically generous, ready for every sacrifice that Christ's love might ask of him. What could have happened? I asked him.

Yes, of course, he still loved Our Lord; he would die for Him; he would even be willing to make all sorts of little sacrifices for Him. . . . But what Jean cannot stand is a whole lot of prohibitions, a sort of " police code " which it seems to him has no connexion with the love of Christ.

No doubt Jean is wrong: all these precepts, these precautions are dictated by the wisdom of experience. Jean has not got this experience, and because he is young he does not want to bow to it. He is wrong, but should he be shut out on this account?

Jean has sworn that he will never again defile a girl; he *knows* he will keep his oath (his certainty is presumptuous, perhaps!). Anyhow he has kept it for a month. Why must he be forbidden to go to camp with a crowd of boys and girls? There's nothing wicked in that.

Jean loves Our Lord, but his vocabulary has not changed with his heart. (It is, I may tell you, highly spiced, full of vitality, but also terribly coarse.) Well, is that going to be called a sin? Can't he talk like the other fellows if he is to be a Christian? Surely Christ, if He's really our brother, if He was a workman himself, surely He'll understand. . . .

Jean was told to fold his hands when he said his prayers! But that is absolutely impossible; that is the mocking sign used in the factory when you want to laugh at priests and show that they're not really men. Can't you be a Christian and still be a real man, a "tough guy"?

Jean wears his cap over one ear and his clothes are flashy— but what harm does that do to Christ? "It seems you can't be a workman if you're a Christian." Religion is, he now feels, a police code. "It's just like the cops."

It took me three months to straighten things out, and Jean made his first Communion with grand fervour. He goes on loving Our Lord, and *bit by bit he finds out for himself* that certain practices stimulate that love; when he has discovered them he does them with all his heart. He is a strange phenomenon among Catholics of the conventional type, but not among the lads of his own world. He has kept his old contacts.

Now Jean is engaged to Suzette. He kisses her conscientiously on the mouth—you kiss a pal or a girl-friend on the cheek, a fiancée on the mouth. Suzette is bringing more refinement into his life, and Jean's religion is gaining insensibly thereby.

The children of this union, who will keep to the path of virtue even if he has to cuff them into it, may find out more refinements of God's love, but I think we shall have to wait for the grandchildren to have a Christianity complete in all its manifestations.

Which ought we to do: preach the Gospel to our pagans, tell them of Christ's love, or expatiate on details of behaviour that seem remote from their lives? If we bring Our Lord to them they understand us. The devotion unto death, the total gift of self asked by religion, holds no fears for them; on the contrary, its *mystique* is powerful in penetrating their lives even if they are not always logical about it (and one might note that logic is not the commonest of gifts—with *any* human being). But if we feel obliged to put up a fight over every detail, we may as well give up. They will never accept a system of morals derived from a categorical imperative or from a law imposed they know not why. But as and when they realise the exigencies of their religion—and the process may be a slow one—they are ready to live the love of Christ in its fullness.

St. Paul's was the first method. He did not win the dockers of Corinth with details of casuistry. The questions he answers in his epistles show that he let consciences be instructed gradually but that all the time he was setting fire to men's hearts by showing them the great truths of revelation. He said that the law must cease to be with Christians the iron weight it had been on the neck of the Jews; he talked of the liberty of the children of God who obey with understanding.

If I grasp St. Paul aright, I think he would have made mass conversions in the factories of Billancourt, Puteaux or Aubervilliers. We French are reproached with our ignorance of geography—do we not also forget history too easily? In the first Christian communities were to be found slaves without rights, without families, without honour, paired off like animals. No more was asked of them at first than they were capable of giving. It is not, I repeat, a question of lowering the demands of the moral law, of omitting some of the precepts, but simply of allowing it to be brought home little by little and of making good use when theology allows of the right to leave people in partial ignorance.

Did not Clovis the King and Charlemagne the Emperor, although really Christians, retain some elements of the uncivilised customs of their age? The Bishops of the time realised that these men had not fully shed the remains of a pagan atavism, and that only after several generations could Christian civilisation be hoped for.

Even among the monks in the finest period of Benedictine monachism a long hereditary paganism sometimes reared its head. There are traces of these wild days in the Ordination ceremony: " If hitherto you have been sluggish in coming to church, now you must be regular. If you have been sleepy, now you must be wide awake. If you have been drunk, now you must be sober; if impure, now chaste." These phrases make us smile today—but they used to be recited in front of the whole congregation in a language understood by them.

Whether we like it or not, our Christianity is tied in with a civilisation. We appreciate the wealth of both religion and civilisation—and the rich culture helps to develop the riches of the Faith. Instinctively, therefore, we tend to make the union closer; we interlace religion and culture, we mingle them to a point at which it seems impossible ever to separate them. We want to pass on the religion and with it to pass on the culture. But have we the right to refuse Christ to those who cannot or will not receive our civilisation? So to act is to imitate the missionaries who want to Europeanise their natives before converting them. Let us offer the Gospel in its nakedness to our proletarian pagans. It will enter their souls and in due course will flower in a culture, different from ours, simpler probably, but genuinely Christian and marvellously adapted to their mentality.

In preaching Christ to these pagans it is hard to set aside all the human values that we have gained with our faith, to make ourselves Jew with the Jews, pagan with the pagans, proletarian with the people. To make abstraction of these values and preach the Faith and the Faith only. When we have immolated all else on the altar of God we hesitate to make this final sacrifice.

But surely this is what St. Paul did. When we think what slavery meant in ancient Rome—no personal rights, no families, no personality even—and when we recall the vast number of slaves in the early Christian communities, we can guess that St. Paul must indeed have preached to them Christ only and Christ crucified.

The masses are ready for the preaching of Jesus crucified if it be given to them without accessories. These words are not just a phrase to give vain encouragement and put a neat end to a paragraph: they are the fruit of personal experience. When you have won a few militants in the pagan world they bring more well-disposed enquirers than you can follow up. And they do not bring them merely to a human friend: they bring them to God's priest. The Gospel ideal stripped of all trimmings is what has made their souls captive.

And, after all, is there not in the demands sometimes made of the proletarian quite a touch of the Pharisee?

A cheating workman is dismissed with great publicity, involving disaster for his future, while honour is paid to a factory owner who underpays his workers and lets immorality go unchecked in his factory.

A navvy is rejected from a religious group because he speaks coarsely, while a chemist who sells birth-control apparatus, more or less openly, is admitted to it.

Even tiny details have a place in painting the picture if we are to see it as a whole. Thus at a recent clergy retreat one of the writers noticed a parish priest with pink enamelled finger-nails. He thought nothing of it: doubtless the priest had been to a manicurist who habitually enamels her customers' nails and who had laid it on, discreetly, even for an ecclesiastic! But why must such severe judgments be passed on a young Catholic laywoman whose nails, too, are enamelled? To hold her place in the world she belongs to, to have any influence in the store she works in, not to be dubbed " old maid ", she must have brightly-coloured nails.

I may be told all this is simply a question of good or bad taste. Granted, and we do not feel ourselves fitted to judge of taste in these matters of the toilet. But did Our Saviour ever demand good taste from His disciples, even from His apostles, before sending them forth to conquer the world?

We have had inside knowledge of many stories of unfaithful wives of prisoners of war! *Before* they fell some of these poor women were cast out with horrified indignation by their parishes—because they appeared to be toying with temptation.

Thus rejected, they were discredited in their own eyes; feeling already lost, they fell more swiftly. Their fellow Christians had abandoned them in their moment of greatest need.

But if we elder brothers are so exigent towards our Christian prodigals, how do we behave towards pagans?

The parable of the Prodigal Son is there to teach us. Our Lord, telling it to the Pharisees, had as His one object to show faith in the mercy of the Father. And the lesson is that if the prodigals do not always return to the Father's house it is not because of the Father. His goodness they know, but His elder sons who have never sinned, who are respectable people, are hard and pitiless.

It may be right to make big demands on Christians—even under pain of excommunication. *But in mission countries pagans are allowed to remain catechumens for a long time while they learn to practise the laws of God* (and to speak of learning and practising implies the possibility of falling, even falling badly). To what proletarian do we give two years, two years of effort, to drag himself out of his paganism?

Half-way House. Intermediate Militants

To become a Christian means to receive also elevation and culture on the human level; and this fact creates a difficulty for our missions that does not arise in far-off lands. For many of our converts, as they become cultivated, rise out of their proletarian condition and even cease to be working-men. The point need not be pressed; so common a fact hardly needs proof; we have only to recall that all the best of our leaders have risen socially after a few years of marriage. And since they rise individually this means of necessity that they change class.

But if they could have risen *in* and *with* an entire popular community (until such time as the condition of the proletariat itself rises) they might have found their natural flowering within that community and they might never have abandoned it. At present they have every right to change, for a man who has the care of a wife and family cannot fairly be asked to maintain them in a lower social condition when they could easily rise higher.

If this is usual among the leaders it is common enough also among the militants. Hence new militants have constantly to be raised up from the masses. When this law is forgotten what happens is that the work, the movement, the sections depending on militants have a period of splendid prosperity after which they tend to decline, sometimes falling very low. For their militants have begun to rise in the world, and little by little, without realising it, they are parting company with their milieu. At first the work carries on through the force of its early impetus, but recruiting comes to an end and very soon that section, that group, will be dead.

Intermediate militants are needed, we depend on them for any considerable numerical increase—and we are almost always without them. We mean people very close to their own milieu, very imperfect, often held still by bad habits, yet sufficiently captured by Our Lord to want to pass on all they have received to their brothers. Some of these have already been described above.

There is danger in sending our good Christian boys and girls into the road houses by the Marne or the little slum cafés. Yet at dances in such places many conversions have been made. Neophytes, who are not yet Christian enough to keep away yet who are Christian enough to be apostles, can do a surprising amount of good.

The same is true in certain camps which are not too healthy, certain mixed groups of boys and girls, certain boarding houses. For all these we need intermediate militants: a saint could not take their place, just as in some cases a priest cannot take the place of a layman. Yet they stir the bile of the " elder brother " and they may make the whole movement suspect in the eyes of respectable people.

Any number of them spring to mind:

the girl who, between two tangos, had the nerve to tell her partner that Christ loved him;

the young woman who, as they waltzed, explained to our friend the boxer her ideal of Christian purity;

the boy who has just been pardoned a multitude of sins, who will fall again through the thousand tyrannies of old habits, yet who bravely confesses Christ in his factory and wins over two comrades;

the youthful group who cannot quite give up fighting but want now to fight for Christ (so they tore up the indecent newspapers on every news-stand in the neighbourhood);

another group who, in the bitter winter of '41-2, when babies were dying for lack of housing and warmth, tore the woollen coats off toy dogs walking on the boulevards with their lady mothers and carried them in triumph to the National Aid headquarters;

the worthy fellow who explained in all simplicity to a chance acquaintance: "Oh no, old man, if you become a Catholic you won't be obliged to go to Mass *every* Sunday. The priests always ask more than they expect to get. I am a real practising Catholic and I go about once a month." Thanks to this width of outlook (!) the friend, too, takes a first step in the way of grace;

the remarried divorcees who are living happily surrounded by children, who have not asked themselves, who will not ask themselves, the question if it is a duty to break up their lives, yet who are helping people to come to Our Lord;

the boy who wanted to improve one of his comrades at a technical school by getting him to regulate his acts of impurity —by spacing them more widely until he was ready to give them up entirely.

All these are intermediate militants—and here are a few more typical examples:

Simone is not a bright girl, but her lack of subtlety breeds in her an astonishing courage. She is ready to " bawl out " her working companions in the bus. Half the members of her section have joined it through her efforts.

Lucienne has set a mark for life on many of her sewing companions in a fashionable establishment. She is only half Christian, but this fact gives her great opportunities in a work-room where Christians had always failed to achieve anything.

Jean was chosen as a leader, yet one day in front of his comrades he thus addressed the pastor: " No kidding, Father, do you really believe in hell and the Devil and the whole bag of tricks? "

Jeannette won Georges for Christ while she was flirting with him. But now Georges is winging his way upwards and has grown too serious for Jeannette, who is starting to flirt with and convert another boy.

Léon went in for black-market operations in the course of which he met Jules and André and won them for Christ to a really profound degree.

I should like to end this catalogue with a story that brought the grace of a real enlightenment to my own mind.

In one area the feminine section of young Christian workers was almost entirely missionary, as the " good girls " of the parish were grouped in another activity. This section enlisted many girls who had not reached the point of going to Mass regularly. During their general assemblies fifteen or twenty young men would be waiting outside the door for their " fiancées ". If the meeting went on too long they would bang on the firmly closed shutters.

Again and again the president suggested that these girls be expelled because of the scandal of these scenes and also the quarrels and jealousies that sometimes came to light: it would have meant throwing out half the section. A reprieve was asked for and granted—especially in the case of a tall blonde called Madeleine.

And then one day a terrible rumour began to get about: Madeleine was going to marry an unbaptised man, a pagan and in a registry office. One of us went to see the young man and discovered the real facts. Madeleine had actually stood out as a Christian against all his solicitations. She had shown him her Jocist badge and said: " No, absolutely, because of this I can't." She had taken a resolution to prepare for her marriage by continence and had for six months utterly abandoned her old bad habits. She had, too, talked so well and so often to the young man that he was ready for baptism. . . . And this was the girl that nobody wanted, the girl that the governing committee of the section had unanimously voted should be expelled.

Of course Christians must not remain permanently in this intermediate state. They must be brought forward slowly if they are unable to advance quickly. But what is very certain is that even while they are incomplete Christians we should get from them all they are able to give.

By this suggestion of half-way militants, we did not mean for an instant that we are prepared to accept a devalued type of Christianity, a Christianity established mainly on a human level. We are conscious of Christ's demands and the limitless nature of the gift He asks. Perhaps indeed we preach this more than others do. Only a profound adaptation of religion to life enables one to see these demands clearly. Catholic Action in a pagan world must be definitely, openly, even spectacularly Christian.

There are in a pagan land pagan *mystiques*. The Church must not baptise these, but must offer the Christian *mystique* in their place. She must adapt it to the actual world, she must incarnate it in their mentality, but what she is offering them is something totally new.

I am not speaking now of the groups with some remains of Christian outlook—these I know less well—but of the pagans. And the pagans are calling on us to preach the Gospel. The task of Catholic Action is two-fold: to help the priest towards opportunities of preaching, and also to participate and collaborate in the direct work of Christianisation.

Father Louis Beinart, who started by a theoretic consideration of this problem, arrived at the same conclusions to which living experience had brought us. He concluded that "traditional Catholicism does not reach the mind" of the pagan proletariat, that therefore Catholics must live among them, learn their language and grasp their outlook and, above all, love them. "An energy of love will make us live the life of our milieu, avoiding only its sins."

But also we must act vigorously on this world. "We must amaze them, we must give them shocks. And this is just what really Christian action does. To manifest love is to startle."

The ineffectiveness of half-way Catholicism emerges plainly enough whenever it is attempted.

In a big Paris hospital a new chaplain was accosted. "Give us some books about morals; the last chaplain only gave us adventure stories, but we knew that wasn't why he came to visit us."

In a factory a worker tried to justify his having four children for all sorts of economic and patriotic reasons. After he had gone the other men said, "Silly goat, everyone knows it's only because he obeys his priests."

At another place a group of young Catholics labelled themselves with some neutral title, but they were the only ones who used it. The others all called them "the young Christians".

One young fellow who was trying to help his fellow workers would talk to them of mutual assistance, of joy, of unity. The man next him whom he was trying to influence asked him point-blank, "Which are you, a Catholic or a Communist?"

Often in the army it was a Protestant who first quoted the Gospels and shifted the discussion onto the religious plane. This often made us feel ashamed, but there was no doubt that this setting the question in its true light made at once for frankness and more open discussion.

Direct Preaching to the Proletarian and Personal Influence

We feel that not enough is done today by way of directly preaching the Gospel to the pagan worker. We realise, not theoretically but practically, that if such preaching is to have

any effect on the masses it must be preceded by a slow working
on the milieu, a gradual lessening of all the pagan influences
that dominate their minds. This is the work of Catholic Action,
but it can be greatly helped by bold and definite preaching.

And in every case a large élite among the proletariat can,
with the help of God's grace, be won to Christianity by preaching, as well today as in the days of St. Paul.

These pagans can be approached directly, not merely by
social and charitable by-ways: these, too, are necessary, but
do not exhaust the possibilities. We have often experienced
the efficacy of direct methods, and we believe that this human
élite, ready to be won by the word of God, could be multiplied
by ten if in the human society that surrounds them were to be
found a real Christian community, no matter how small, which
by its very presence posed the question of religion ("See how
they love one another").

And again, as to preaching we feel that lay action, while
indispensable, is not sufficient to bring to the practices of religion
all these profoundly pagan folk, especially the adults. Even
when successful lay action is slow, it does a wonderful work
of preparation, it brings men near the Church, but there is a
certain risk of their getting started off on a road as it were
parallel with Christianity which fails to join it at the point of
religious practice, unless this preparation is supplemented
by preaching. The priest must, of course, adapt his sermons
carefully to their minds and then the grace of the priesthood
itself ensures that the Holy Spirit will complete His work.

It need hardly be said that the presentation of doctrine must
be re-thought with the utmost care if it is to find its way to
these neo-pagan souls.

A Real Understanding of the Church.

What priest has not felt a deep and urgent necessity to give
to his community a keener sense of the Church, adding thereby
to all his other methods of Christian training the chief of all:

life lived in a brotherhood of mutual affection and religious interdependence? We have both been made specially conscious of this need through our efforts to form Christian proletarian communities. We have come to think, moreover, that these groups may well do more than many sermons to give an impetus to some of our rather fossilised congregations and even serve them as models. It is hard for the Catholic who has not even momentarily experienced—nay who has not actually lived—this life of the Church to realise it imaginatively.

In periods of high development it is in those parts of the nation least affected that the fundamental needs of humanity are most keenly felt. Elsewhere they are smothered by the unrealities and artificialities of life, but there is in the proletariat a most tremendous urge (increasingly perceptible the lower you go) of primitive natures thirsting for the community of which they have been robbed by the great industrial urban concentrations. This is one of the chief causes, little as it has been grasped, of the Socialist and Communist triumphs. The word " comrade " has a content for the workman of a mystical depth that we are far from fully understanding. Young proletarians live in community; we must win them in groups; it is in clusters that they will cling to Christ, the living vine.

Our boxer brought with him all his pupils (and gave us for good measure boxing lessons at the J.O.C.). He brought, too, his group of girl fans—for every boxer has a little bevy of admiring girls. Twenty-seven of these boys and girls were seized with enthusiasm for Our Lord as their Ideal.

Elsewhere a group who danced together every Sunday began to feel a vague religious stirring which led them at last to seek out a priest.

And here is a pleasant story. A dozen good fellows got together with the highly humanitarian object of inviting ugly girls to dances, girls who got " fed up " and sick of life because no one ever invited them. This team again was captured as a whole and asked to be transformed into a Christian community.

Josette (some of whose " Christian " exploits would not bear telling) is at the head of a band—she is strong through her leadership, and the same is true of René.

You might think from some of our stories that individual conversions are the rule. There are such on higher proletarian levels, but the young of the real proletariat always go about in bands, and to possess the leader is to possess the band.

In thinking of the profounder depths of these popular communities a comparison is suggested with the first century of the Church's life. We see something happening today that may enable us to understand what happened in an age not unlike our own, especially as to its pagan proletariat.

Friendship is in the lives of our proletarian converts more than an accessory or a means, more in their eyes even than an end. *To be a friend is to be a Christian.* Friendship among themselves, friendship with Christ, considered with deep reverence yet as one of themselves. They indeed demonstrate to us that absolute oneness which makes the two great commandments like unto one another.

Wonders can be accomplished in such an atmosphere! What results have we not seen from the furnace of Christian love that pervades it, results not rare but frequent. Converts have been known to break at once and without relapse with the bad habits of a lifetime, drunkenness, impurity, sinful connections, even theft. Poor fellows less gifted develop beyond any recognition and become in this Christian community able to achieve results far beyond their strength.

My fellow priests will bear me witness that we have felt deeply conscious of the breath of the Holy Spirit. One priest was simply overwhelmed by a speech Bertrand made to his comrades about the Holy Ghost and came to ask if I had helped him. Bertrand had prepared his subject and then, he said, " I chewed it over as I rolled my barrow through the streets ". He is a newsboy, baptised a little while ago, not yet confirmed. But a doctor of theology declared that the talk had brought him light.

Obviously this mystical tendency is not without its dangers if it remains outside the Church. The remedy is not to kill the spirit in all these souls, to annihilate these young communities, but rather to integrate them into the Church. They have, alas, their less noble aspects, but the life-giving Spirit is among them and strengthening them. The Church would gain an untold treasure in making them her own.

CATHOLIC MISSIONARY ACTIVITY

Why the Jocist Movement has not yet succeeded in establishing Proletarian Missions

THE question asked at this point will be whether the Jocists, with all their ramifications, male and female groups, married groups, etc., have not taken this work in hand. Surely we may hope that little by little they will transform and christianise the proletariat.

The answer was prophetically given by Paul Hibout, an early Jocist propagandist, in the form of a question to Mgr. Richard, auxiliary Bishop of Versailles:

" We are ready for tomorrow—but are you ready for the day after?

" We are ready, we of the workers' Catholic Action, to make a dent in the proletarian world. But will you be ready to gather into the Christian world the enquirers we bring to you— and to keep them there? "

This book gives the answer. No, the Church in France was not ready for the day after tomorrow. It had not the organisation. Here lies the chief cause why these missions have not come into being. Everyone sees it and we certainly have no intention of denying it. Catholic Action has not yet bitten into the pagan proletariat, and in the actual conditions of our ministry it appears unable to do so. In saying this I am speaking of powerful movements that express the proletariat as a whole, not of interesting sporadic experiments lacking any future.

Paul Hibout might well say today, " We do not choose to begin again tomorrow unless you will get ready for the day after. The advance guard is in danger if the army is not close behind it."

Using a phrase that expresses the Church's universality we may say that the " sound " of the Jocist movement has " gone forth " even to the depths of the proletarian world—and that is quite an achievement, it is the proof of a dynamic adolescence. But Catholic Action among the workers must come of age if it is to pervade the world of the workers—and for this we need missions and a missionary clergy.

For what is the J.O.C. but the first wholly workers' movement meaning by workers' movement a movement of the masses? Hitherto Catholic youth movements, aware of their relatively small numbers, aspired only at winning a chosen few, hoping always, of course, that these few, once trained, would do their work on the masses. But the J.O.C. aims directly (where these others aimed only indirectly) at enrolling and organising the masses.

" This means that in a certain sense the J.O.C. is itself something new in the Church's history in being actually a ' class ' movement. Not the movement of one class against another, not a movement engaged in class warfare, yet still a class movement, or, more accurately, the movement of one social milieu. The existence of various social worlds is a fact of which we cannot be unaware. His own society is the world in which a man has his natural growth and development. It is the air that he breathes; it is that human framework in which his whole life is set; it is for him the concrete and immediate expression of human fellowship—it is his world. In this world he must live; in it he must save his soul. Our problem is not that of maintaining a few young people for two or three hours a week in an artificial world entirely distinct from their own. It is rather that of maintaining the young worker in his natural world, in his own class and enabling him to transform that class, the class of the workers, the proletarian world."[1]

[1] This quotation from Georges Hoog's *Histoire du Catholicisme social en*

The strength in France of the young Christian workers is well known. Eighty thousand gathered in 1937 in the Parc des Princes, the southern federal meeting of 1942 numbered one hundred thousand. They have influenced the clergy and the entire Church of France and they have communicated a splendid enthusiasm to Christians beyond the frontiers of France. But although in our great cities there are groupings of varying success in the world of the parish, there is nothing effective or organised among the pagan proletariat. And this is not for lack of effort. The J.O.C. was created for the pagans; it is missionary of its very essence; it has struggled for ten years, trying every method, beginning afresh after every failure. But its work has always come to a dead end for the reason given above—a missionary movement cannot exist without a missionary community, and this community is lacking. That the parish is not this community is no matter of reproach: it is not within its power.

Yet have we not cause for some degree of self-reproach as we examine what is lacking? Can we honestly say that Pius XI's directives on Catholic Action have been listened to and carried out? He says, for instance:

" Catholic Action is a true apostolate in which all Catholics should share without distinction of sex, culture or social condition " (Letter *Quae Nobis*, 1928).

" The various branches of Catholic Action should not be fused but co-ordinated in such a way as to constitute an organic body made up of parts, distinct from one another but all contributing to a unique vitality " (Discourse, 1930).

" To bring back to Christ all the different kinds of men that have rejected him, apostles are needed who understand the outlook of their own world. The direct apostles of the workers will be workers, those of the commercial and industrial world will be men in commerce and industry " (*Quadragesimo Anno*, 1931).

France refers to the J.O.C. so finely described by Van der Meersch in his novel, *Fishers of Men*. But how many groups are like that of Mardyck and Dhouthulst?

Setting aside all the publicity, the sentimental outpourings (and there have been plenty), let us ask ourselves how movements of specific Catholic Action are *in practice* started in parishes.

They are in practice added on to the existing good works: Children of Mary, Eucharistic Crusade, youth and sporting groups, St. Vincent de Paul, Ladies of Charity. One suburban rector remarked to the present writer, " I have twenty-three good works in my parish now. You think that a J.O.C.F. would be useful. Good. I am perfectly willing. That makes twenty-four good works." And he wrote it down on his list.

But is the movement specifically designated as Catholic Action simply to be counted as one in a list of good works? The question need hardly be asked. How then can we seriously hope that Catholic Action thus understood—in fact merely tolerated—will flourish and produce results?

All the same, the J.O.C., as far as a limited experience goes, has had a magnificent success, and this largely thanks to the clergy. The young workers of the parish are deeper and more genuine Christians, they have a greater spirit of conquest and they convert every year some of their comrades, bringing them out of the pagan world into the world of the parish. This apostolate awakens a spirit of more generous Christianity in our good boys, but it is inside the parish, it does not affect *at all* the missionary problem. This problem, we say again, clearly, categorically, this missionary problem cannot be solved by parish priests overwhelmed with work, enslaved to a tiny Christian community which jealously swallows them up.

Let us look at an instance of this. The XVIIIth arrondissement of Paris contains two hundred and eighty-five thousand inhabitants: about thirty thousand young workers, fourteen to twenty-five years old: *four* Jocist sections. One of these tries to remain within the proletariat of the Boulevard Ney. Thanks to the wonderful devotion of their priest, they do manage to hold on. They consist of fifteen Jocists, six of whom are militants. Another section has neither chaplain nor meet-

ing-place, yet it boasts eight militants and twenty associates.
The third in the Oeuvre de Championnet has ten older
militants and forty younger, but no Jocists of between eighteen
and twenty-five. The fourth section simply gets together the
young Catholics of one parish. These four sections are a valuable addition for the Christian groups they serve; they help
to keep in the Church some of the young workers. Priests
devote themselves, the young laity half kill themselves with
work, and some splendid Christians emerge.

Side by side with the boys the girl Jocistes have five sections:
Championnet with twenty-seven members of whom ten are
militants; St. Bernard thirty-seven associates and fifteen
militants; St. Denis six associates, three militants; Ste. Hélène
ten associates, six militants—and one fine militant at St. Pierre
who is getting something going.

The L.O.C. has one men's section forming and a second
which they share with the XVIIth arrondissement. It brings
together ten male militants and twenty female. A section of
young married couples has a dozen militant families.

All this represents a great volume of work. But take a look
at the problem of the two hundred and thirty thousand pagans
of the district and you will see that it is not and it can never
be by promoting these parochial sections which have been going
now some ten or twenty years that satisfactory results can be
obtained.

If we turn to non-practising areas where a Christian culture
remains we can see the counter-proof of this. It is a complete
change of perspective. Even inside the framework of the
parish the J.O.C. becomes numerically strong. The town of
Lille, which has about the same number of inhabitants as the
XVIIIth arrondissement, can claim in its area six federations
of Jocists with sixty-five sections—and this does not count
the other groups. Yet Lille, too, has a mass of untouched
proletarians.

The conclusion to be drawn is surely this: the various groups
of young Christian workers *are striving with all their energies*

to be real missionaries among the pagan proletariat. But they cannot succeed apart from missions.

This discovery, resulting from the fifteen years' life of the workers' movement, explains why Catholic Action within the pagan proletariat has had so meagre a success. We know that some consider that the fault lies entirely with our parochial organisation. We consider this unjust. *We narrow the possibilities of the parish to that which really lies in its power. We do not blame it for failing to do what it could not possibly have accomplished.*

Both of us have experience of the parochial ministry: it gets hold of a man body and soul, it devours him, it possesses him to the point where he simply cannot think of anything else. We know all about it and we are anxious to set down in this book how great are the devotion and self-sacrifice called for by this ministry.

Necessity of Catholic Missionary Activity

Must we then suppress in our parishes the organisations of Catholic Action? Nobody is making such a suggestion! To rob them of a wonderful means of training, to cut short this burst of renewal and deepening of religion so often to be found in them is not to be thought of. It would mean taking away from our parishes all those chosen groups which are their pride and their joy.

It is said that you must judge the education given to the young by what they make of it. Such a judgement can be formed only after they are settled in life. Experience in the diocese of Paris of the " jeunes foyers " (young Christian households) is instructive. These young couples come from all sorts of Catholic groups, but only the specialised Catholic Action movements, the scouts and the " City of God " give any preparation that is effective in producing families likely to live as Christians and to carry out the obligations of Christian marriage. There are, of course, exceptions, due to the influence of a family or a priest educator, but these exceptions only prove the rule.

Parochial Catholic Action is tremendously important for another reason. Today all the Catholic forces, *all* the Catholic forces, must be organised closely and intelligently if they are to gain influence over political, civic, social and economic affairs. Without this action on the institutions and on the main streams of national life no conquest of the masses is possible and all the work discussed here becomes almost useless. The forces of evil are marvellously well organised, our troops must be the same. " A good Catholic " from a parish who refuses to join a general movement is a traitor to the cause.

No, parochial Catholicism must not be suppressed, but intensified. In our missionary areas it must also be adapted, sometimes to a very great degree, adapted that it may become the leaven in the parochial dough—for the parish, too, needs renewal.

There is apt to be some confusion between the parochial outlook and that of the Federation of Catholic Action which indicates the elements of this problem. The directives of the federal committee are given with a missionary Jocism in view. When the parish tries to carry them out there is a grinding of the machinery, the thing doesn't work and the chaplains are conscious of this.

In one town where an effort was made to establish a Jocist section the parochial youth who were on a higher social level felt they did not fit into a definitely workers' association. They left the J.O.C. (which might have adapted itself to their group) and started the movement called " Unité ". It was an immense success and shaped the boys and girls of the parish into a marvellous dynamic Christian community. Their flaming zeal will soon have conquered the whole parish. Lately they sought out the Jocist federation and said to them, " Our movement is going strong, but it does not touch the proletarians. They remain to be conquered and we would like you to start a Jocist section for them. We will help it from a distance; we will rent a shop in town for a meeting place, etc. . . . "

The departures for Germany put an end to this fine scheme. But it could have been carried out, thanks to these lay missionaries, who were willing to stand the expenses and then efface themselves before the " native " laity whenever they should come forward.

We do not want to lay down lines of possible adaptations, but only to remark that they could be handled so as to put an end to many difficulties. There still remains the need for a missionary Catholic Action directly adapted for pagans.

Let us look at this in the light of a problem of the immediate future.

Supposing the State organises our youth, it will make use of existing educational movements, it will bless the creation of new movements, will supplement the deficiencies by creating one especially for " those who are left out ", an idea with which we are in full sympathy. But how will the whole thing work out in practice?

At Villedieu-en-Blouère (you remember that little Catholic village we spoke of ?) everything will be wonderful. With a handful of exceptions all the young are united in a quasi-official and powerfully Christian movement. At another place, of Christian culture although non-practising, Fons le Saunier, things do not promise quite so well. There are three or four concurrent movements in existence and this always results in a little unfriendly rivalry, at any rate among the young.

But what about our pagan Paris arrondissement? What difference will it make if the thirty thousand young workers are divided among two or three movements! We Christians would certainly not get together a thousand young people from all the different parishes and yet we are far better off there than in most places, thanks to the immense labours of the Championnet Centre. We shall have about thirty good Jocist militants to form a nucleus with about as many really Christian leaders brought in from outside. Not very many for a movement that shall represent to the world Christ, the Church and the ideals of the Gospel. And what of the mass of twenty-nine thousand left without any Gospel leaven? *Is not Catholic Action on them a necessity—a Catholic Action that is missionary?*

Perhaps it will be said that the same youth could be at once the nucleus of the Christian movement and at the same time the leaven in the other movements. Such a remark is a grim sort of jest. Could the Jocist militants in the Catholic schools become also Christian propagandists in the State schools? To ask such a question is to answer it.

Another Problem of Catholic Action. The Problem of Numbers

A serious criticism often formulated against Catholic Action, and more specifically against the specialised movements, is this: Their method, although admirably designed to create marvellous prototypes for the Christianity of a new age, is only satisfactory in bringing together a small number and does not manage to get at big numbers *even of existent Christian communities.* These communities, made up of weak, routine Christians, need to be supported, brought into line, converted to something better.

On this point it is worth observing that every new movement must lay deep and solid foundations before spreading out. This is even more true of a movement that will in the end be called upon to extend far and wide, and we know the place that Catholic Action is on the road to filling in the Church's organisation.

The Council of Trent had not achieved all its results by the end of the sixteenth century. We must not forget that Catholic Action is a young movement. This fact does not answer the criticism, but it does narrow its field. The question is a complex one and the distinctions we have drawn will help to cast light on it.

In all the areas of the second type—of a Catholic culture, although not of practising Catholics—the criticism is simply untrue. Whenever the specific movements of Christian Action are run as they should be, are aided by the clergy in the measure of their importance, the results in these areas are quite amazing.

At Flers, for instance, the Family Movement reaches nine-tenths of the prisoners' wives and the provisions of workers' gardens made by it affects half the working population. This is a typical, not an isolated, case: I could cite many others, indeed, wherever such results are *not* achieved I could indicate the precise reasons for partial failure, with, however, these reservations:

(1) Very few middle-sized or even small towns are without a larger or smaller proportion of that pagan proletariat which poses a totally different problem.

(2) The adults have sometimes still kept a Christian outlook and are now widely separated from other Christians—while the young are more pagan, are indeed already almost inaccessible to Christianity.

When we turn to the pagan proletariat with which this book is concerned, we do not deny, we agree with the criticism on Catholic Action. We accept the facts alleged—and we are trying to explain them. The principal responsibility lies on the organisation of the apostolate in these areas: but, having said that, we freely admit that Catholic Action by the workers has not yet discovered its appropriate formula. To me it seems that *it is not sufficiently specialised.* This statement will appear surprising: it is strictly accurate, but it needs explaining.

In order not to part company with the masses, a workers' section of the J.O.C. refuses to be wholly identified with the closed world of the parish. Yes, it does desire to be something separate, it desires to be a mission. But all alone, with no missionary clergy, no missionary set-up, how can it succeed?

The basis of the Catholic Action apostolate, the basis of all total Christianity, of all apostolate to the masses, is the same, " the leaven in the dough". This must mean Christians staying in their own world to redeem it, staying fully *of* their world in all that is not sin. And as we have seen, human associations are formed in a definite society, they create a society, and true community can exist only between people of the same society . . . an elementary educational formula.

One of the present writers was for a long time chaplain of the J.O.C.F. section of Perreux where a perfect community had been formed, made up of maids and saleswomen from the big shops. Little by little the maids became alienated from their own world and ceased to influence it. The saleswomen, on the other hand, would not dare to bring the friends from their department into a section partly composed of servants. They themselves, being deeply Christian, were willing to come, but from new aspirants towards conversion they could not ask almost heroic courage. The end of it was that two groups had to be formed, one for the saleswomen, the other for the maids.

Whether you like it or not, any group, Catholic Action or not, denominated " specialised " or not, *specialises itself* and becomes a certain type of society.

In what good work, what association, what Third Order—if living in a real community of life, not merely coming together for occasional meetings—will you find working women and lady companions, engineers and scavengers?

How in the present condition of our parishes can numbers be got at in such very varied worlds? There are, we repeat, whole areas of human activity in the proletariat of all large cities where Christ is not and cannot be preached. If all these worlds are to hear the Gospel, meetings of militants must be multiplied and remultiplied—we must specialise more and more.

We find ourselves facing certain sociological laws which, if not as easy to state as the law of gravity, are quite as certain in their action: a basic community will acquire more members the more specialised it is; and the corollary to it: the greater number of diversified types in a basic community the sooner it will reach the limit of expansion possible to it.

If in our towns we are only to have communities of fifty to sixty families no specialisation is needed. But if we have two thousand, five thousand, and, even more, if we have thirty to sixty thousand members, specialisation is essential. Even a community of two thousand of different cultures has been proved impossible over and over again. A country priest with ten children to instruct can easily handle them, however various in their education and upbringing; a curate in Paris with one to two hundred children can only instruct those who are prepared to understand him, those whose training has been of a similar sort. A class of ten children of vastly differing quality can be handled, but a class of fifty is impossible unless they have been learning in the same educational world.

A parish of sixty families forms a real community out of landowners, farmers and shopkeepers. To try to create such a community in a district of a great city would be to limit it to a few hundred families, and even then . . .

Facing an increasingly complicated world the apostolate becomes complicated. This may not be what one would wish, but it is a fact. You cannot fight sociological laws with idealist dreams, however beautiful and mystical. Specialised Christian communities are needed in our huge and deeply diversified societies. In affirming this we are not, like many of our contemporaries, failing to feel the urge of the Holy Spirit towards Church unity. We think, on the contrary, that through these communities we shall re-discover the wealth and youth of the faith. There must be also certain non-specialised communities in areas where specialisation is not required. Some of these will go very far in becoming types and witnesses of that great power of the Church that we call her Unity. This *mystique* of unity will itself be one of the foundations of our much desired missions. But it must be incarnated in life as it is really lived and must take account of its exigencies.

To incarnate a *mystique* in reality is not to diminish it but to bring it back to life.

Reply to Criticisms of Specialisation

We know that in the ears of some of our contemporaries the word specialisation strikes an offensive note: to them it sounds like 1939, strangely pre-war. Do we not realise better today (they feel) the unity that should come through membership of the Mystical Body of Christ?

For heaven's sake let us clear up this confusion. A body is not disunited because it is diversified. It need not be all arms, and all right arms at that, or all feet and those the same feet, so that we may say, "It is one". Do we want to correct St. Paul?

No, indeed, the more complex a body is, the more special organs it has, the more those organs can rejoice in their common life. The Church is universal and the boundaries of the nations do not damage its unity. There are varieties of culture, too, which are no less important than geographical varieties, but which damage the unity of the Church no more than they do. On the contrary, the Christian affirmation of unity will only be made in its fullness when Christian communities become richly vital just because they are so specialised, so well fitted to the need they fill.

His Holiness Pius XII urges us to study the early Christians and we must try to understand what he means: he does not tell us to imitate all that the early Christians did, but he clearly indicates the value of looking back at our beginnings.

Let us try to extract a lesson for ourselves from the life of the early Church.

The Greatest Common Denominator among the Early Christians

The first fact that sticks out among the ardent converts of the primitive Church is the love that animated their communities and enabled them to transcend all the differences of social conditions. If from this fact the conclusion be drawn that the differences separating men of various social worlds are smaller than the differences between the cultures considered in the abstract, we entirely agree, we have said so already. There is less difference between a real bourgeois and a workman, both for some time engaged in the same good work, than between this workman living in the parochial world and his completely proletarian neighbour; it is easier to bring the first two into one community than the second two.

Yet two points must be emphasised: (a) The first Christians were all converts, therefore on the whole of one world, (b) Yet even so we soon see them split into two communities which it took some effort to unite. There were the Judaisers who might be compared with those today in the habit of religious practice. These were, and are, more easily " justified " by outward works. The pagan converts had more dynamism, and even sometimes gifts of prophecy, but seem to have fallen oftener into sin.

Even at that time one of the apostles specialises in the conversion of the heathen, which does not mean that he rejects the others.

In St. Paul's communities one is deeply conscious of these two groups, fused with difficulty, until the numbers of the Jews diminish, giving place to Christians who had all been converted from paganism.

Note further that at its beginnings the Church could not do everything at once and no great effort was made to adapt the Christian message to each state of life. We possess no details on special ways of being a Christian slave, a Christian soldier, a Christian aristocrat—all we hear about is certain cases of conscience that had to be resolved.

The realisation of all the wealth of adaptation that Christianity possesses was to be the work of later generations. At the beginning the joy of having found Christ pushed everything else into the background. Later came the consideration of methods whereby the ideal should permeate the whole of life.

There is nothing surprising in this. Converts are not always logical, they are mystical rather than pragmatic. It is only later that experience gives us Ignatian or Salesian spirituality, the spiritualities that belong to Christendom.

How did the Early Christian Communities come into being?

We know very little of the apostolic age from this angle. It may be that when the numbers of the faithful were small the type of the community was the family. No *problem* of specialisation would then arise, for the family is actually an example of advanced specialisation: each member has his own office specially adapted to him.

Some historians think that the meetings alluded to by St. Paul could not have been adequate for the Corinthian Christians, could not possibly have brought them all together. It is hard to imagine even an assembly of one hundred on the model described by St. Paul, with a meal in common, with prophecies, interpretations and the rest. And there can hardly have been as few as one hundred Christians at Corinth. Some are of opinion that this assembly was a sort of general religious meeting attended in rotation to insure unity, much as Jocist sections meet at the Federation. They believe that the domestic assemblies, historically to be found in the period immediately following, were already in existence.

Again, the idea that Christians normally assembled in the narrow damp passages of the Catacombs is a legend that is luckily disappearing. The meetings took place in the house of some one who had a big enough room; the militant gathered his friends together, his neighbours, his customers. It was absolutely the natural groupings of the J.I.C. before its time! But with more paternalism, of course, for the little ones and the slaves who were still in a state of absolute dependence. Each one of these little groups had its own character, its special stamp, its own " climate ".

Our world is, of course, more complex than that of ancient Rome, and its special needs must be borne in mind. There are a thousand reasons why we should adapt ourselves to the techniques of our own age and take full account of existing divisions. It is no use trying to fight with guerilla troops against the armoured divisions of an army in fine fighting fettle.

The important thing is to draw lessons from our *real* likenesses to the early Church, those points in which we can most clearly note its spirit.

(1) There must be *real* Christian communities, i.e. relatively small, where they all know one another and throw into the common stock their efforts at a supernatural way of living.

(2) There should be special groups for neophytes, a real catechumenate which takes them as they are and educates them gradually, each one according to his capacity and the demands of grace on him.

(3) Each of these communities must be impregnated by extremely warm, extremely enthusiastic friendship, to give to all a human idea of the marvellous divine unity of the Mystical Body.

(4) These communities should not be made up exclusively of young or old or of adults, nor be exclusively male or female, for in such groups is no hope of permanence. They should be natural communities, grouping families as a whole.

(5) As far as human weakness allows, these communities should feel deeply united among themselves, going towards the same end under the guidance of a leader. But this does not exclude closer links within each community between those specially drawn towards one another by human inclination and tenderness.

(6) This union carries with it a participation in common in the same liturgy.

All these manifestations explain the " See how they love one another " uttered so often concerning the early Church. For what amazed the pagans was chiefly the love that reigned inside each community.

Early Christians still exist, and we have heard this same

thing often today. Out of hundreds of converts we questioned (not marriage converts) three-quarters were captured through the friendliness of the little Christian groups they got among. There are still *Christian communities of the primitive Church* and they attract young souls marvellously, only we have to *keep these communities*. There is our problem.

Lay Catholic Action

In existent communities the Church's task is to make Christianity all-embracing, to make it more personal, penetrating every activity of life. The Church must also gather all Christians together into a mighty army.

This calls for Catholic Action within the ecclesiastical framework; in these communities, as elsewhere, the priest needs help so that he can give his entire time to work that he alone can do.

Both children and adults, if they are to hold out against the pagan influences of the Press, the radio, the cinema etc., must receive a solid and very personal Christian training. This requires many lay teachers, men and women.

Then, too, there are areas of life which are in varying degrees outside the priest's power of participation: the factory, leisure employments, love and engagement, the intimacies of marriage. The renewal must actually come about through the profound sanctification of this entire secular life. Catholic Action is utterly indispensable for this: it is the new blood which will give back their vigour to these Christian communities.

In non-practising areas of Christian culture this great task is doubled: the few real Christians must become a dynamic and fertile leaven doing their work upon the dough. But for the greater number it is a matter of bringing them to a full practice of their religion—practice both of the law of charity and of what are specifically called " religious practices ".

The influence of human respect in these areas is vast. The priest can do nothing unless an example is given by young men and women, by fiancés like the rest, married couples like the rest, but not afraid to bear witness to Christ. Fallen-away Catholics are perhaps more afraid of the priest than are pagans; as soon as they see him coming they begin to fear he will drag them back to Mass and Confession. They are terrified to set foot inside the club—the " patro ". They went there as children, then one fine day when they were adolescent they left. Certainly the priest by himself can't rebuild all these ruins. There must be Catholic Action teams, there must be households who bring Christ back into their own world and persuade that world to receive Christ's priest.

Without Catholic Action movements that can bring together not only convinced Christians but also youths and adults of a Christian outlook, a priest may as well prepare to read the burial service over the Christianity in his parish. It will drag on a little longer, growing weaker and weaker, and then will die like a patient in a decline.

In the proletarian missions the burden of the work must lie on the shoulders of Catholic Action. Here, above all, it is abundantly clear that the priest by himself can do little. The milieu is too far away from him.

It is hard to see how he can work effectively by himself on the pagan world of our big cities. He doesn't know the milieu, he doesn't belong to it; in any event it is too vast for the handful of priests we have. The priest needs interpreters, for he is in a country the language and habits of which are unknown to him. He will only be accepted by that world if he is introduced by natives, by " right guys ".

From what has been said above it should be clear enough that there is no question here of Catholic Action, however strongly developed, as it now operates inside the parish. There must be a mission and a missionary Catholic Action.

For Heaven's sake do not let us lay upon our Catholic Action sections educated in the parochial milieu the impossible task of carrying out a mission all by themselves. Let us not discourage these young folk. We have seen enough to know that, left to themselves, lacking missionary priests, lacking missionary preaching, lacking missionary organisations, lacking missionary worship, they cannot possibly achieve great and lasting results.

Surely we must say of Catholic Action among the workers what Pius XI said in 1922 of the foreign missions: the problem is the same. Hitherto we have been using a fishing rod. Now we must begin to win whole worlds for Christ—the milieu with its masses.

" A great number of souls have been saved, great glory has been given to God, but how many are still being lost? For how many souls is the blood of the Redeemer shed in vain? There remain whole populations in their vast masses. . . . These masses are still waiting for the words of salvation."

These words were spoken in St. Peter's on Whit Sunday, 1922, in a sermon on the Propagation of the Faith. The Pope went on to show that " side by side with that defence of the Faith which preserves the treasures of Christian life there must be conquests carrying everywhere the light of the Gospel and the holiness of the Christian law, and begetting new children for the Church".

The great scandal of the Church in the nineteenth century, Pius XI said to Canon Cardijn, was not that she lost many workers but that she lost " the working classes ". Cannot we at least begin the work of bringing this scandal to an end?

BEFORE proceeding further we must answer a difficulty felt by many. "We quite agree with you," they say, "but where are the priests to be found for all this extra work?"

Put thus, the question is unanswerable. To answer it we should be obliged to question the necessity of certain organisations and activities that are regarded as sacrosanct by too many people for us to dare to touch them. We shall therefore answer only by setting out certain facts, making certain comparisons, some of which may point towards solutions—though we shall not try to specify methods in detail.

We begin by insisting again that a missionary clergy is a necessity. The duty of so insisting has been brought home to us by ten years of attempts, difficulties, frustrations and mis-understandings. We have seen too many of our youth wounded and crushed by the impossible task of conquering the prole-tariat with the arms with which we have furnished them. We want to put an end to these fruitless and discouraging attempts.

True, the conquest of the proletariat is "a matter for mili-tants", but it is also *a matter for the clergy*. If starting without militants is risky, there is danger also in starting without a specialised clergy for this task, a real missionary clergy.

Without a priest to follow up each experiment, how can the demands of Christianity be safely adapted to this new world; how can men under the powerful and disturbing outpourings with which God's spirit favours them be guided and governed? How can those serious mistakes be prevented which might ruin everything and which a few enthusiastic priests might all too easily make, swept away by their lay leaders and hardly know-ing in what direction they are going? No, the work cannot be a matter of retouching here, replastering there, adapting this or that detail.

An event that occurred recently paints a faithful picture of the way we desert our militants because we have no missions to support them.

Pierre was gaining an excellent livelihood for himself and his wife (he had been some time married) at a factory where he had started a Catholic Action group among the workers. By mass methods and pamphlets designed for the masses he managed to gather more than one hundred active members, boys, young men, young women: about a third of the concern. They were not yet a Christian group, but the first stirrings might be felt and the Holy Spirit was working in these souls.

The food having become utterly insufficient in the factory dining-room, the personnel petitioned the management, in a quite respectful fashion, and this young group took charge of negotiations. The only answer was the establishment of a separate dining-room for the management, which removed the last hope of an improvement. The personnel then decided to demonstrate: by taking up their stand, watching in absolute silence, as the management came out of their dining-room. The young neophytes took part in this demonstration which consisted only of their presence and their silence.

But the next night an anarchist tried to set the room on fire—little damage was done, but the excitement was considerable.

Pierre was accused, questioned, dragged before the police, treated as a criminal. In the police court he confessed Christ. Reproached for having some queer specimens in his group, including a girl of easy virtue, he declared that he wanted to win them for Christ and that he was himself ready to suffer for Christ. " Christ is my leader," he said.

They laughed at him and treated him as a fanatic. Our world, to be sure, is no longer accustomed, is not yet re-accustomed, to this kind of Christianity. Nothing could be fastened on him, but he was dismissed from the factory in disgrace. And that was the end of his chances; he could hardly hope for another job. Good-bye to the monthly four thousand francs which allowed him to hope for an easier future.

What could we do for him? Absolutely nothing.

The religious authorities could not, of course, defend as Christians people who were not yet Christians. They could hardly risk the destruction of the larger movement of Catholic Action for the sake of one man or even for a group of a hundred neophytes.

We are not geared to the establishment of missions in the factories.

With the Host at my Mass this morning I offered up the immense sacrifice made by Pierre and his wife. I offered it to Our Lord with all my soul as a priest, but I was distracted during my thanksgiving. I was asking myself, " Have we the right to send missionaries among the proletariat before we have planned and organised missions? "

After this glance at the problem itself let us look at a few facts bearing on the question of the clergy.

Poligny (Jura) is a little town of some three thousand three hundred, all but a few hundred of them members of the Christian community. The parish priest and his two assistants have plenty of work; their lives are full, but they are not harassed and overwhelmed and they have plenty of time to go after the few wanderers from the parochial fold.

The parish of St. Vincent de Paul at Clichy has also three thousand, St. Eloi in Paris has eighteen hundred—and we could mention many parishes with about that number of " practising " Catholics. The urban communities are for the most part less fervent than Poligny. There are fewer confessions, fewer sick calls—and yet in these parishes six, seven or even more priests are absolutely overwhelmed with work.

It looks as though the greater part of the labours of three or four priests is absorbed not by missionary work but by very secondary occupations: the burial of people nine-tenths of whom did not receive the Last Sacraments, or marriages which have little chance of lasting, clubs and even catechism for a crowd of children who most certainly will never reappear after their first Communion. These are not useless forms of apostolate, yet one can think of others far more useful.

If we tried to make a timetable of the occupations of the various priests in a town parish, would we be sure to find all their time filled by the most priestly, the most apostolic kinds of work?

How many hours go to waste in making arrangements for marriages and funerals and such matters, from which the priest could usefully be released for his real and serious work. And again the curate deputed to look after the finances simply becomes an accountant, while the sacristan might as well be the employee of a furniture warehouse. And the director of various parish activities, with his management, his projects, his skill in bringing things off, appears sometimes more like a business man than a preacher of the Gospel. Surely the Bishop did not ordain them for such occupations as these?

If only we could achieve a saner outlook and a better regulation of the order of values in our various activities: first preaching the Gospel and giving the sacraments, then the ceremonies of worship, lastly administration.

All this would come about if we followed Pius XI's directive in his encyclical *Divini Redemptoris* (March 19, 1937): " Every other good work, however beautiful, however useful, must give place to the vital need of saving the very foundations of Christian faith and civilisation. Let the parish priests . . . reserve their greatest strength and the largest share of their energy to win back the masses of the workers to Christ and to the Church and to gain an entry for Christianity among those who are most remote from it."

A simple parallel between France and the mission countries may well conclude this section of our study.

France contains in city areas some eighteen million inhabitants, of whom more than nine million belong to the pagan proletariat. Our Catholic colleges employ several thousand priests and religious (some entirely on the business side). If half of these were working as missionaries, France would not revert to paganism, and the recruitment of priests would increase.

In 1931 an article in the *Bulletin des anciens élèves de Saint Sulpice* raised this very question and discussed how the missionary spirit could be exercised in the parochial ministry. This article seems to have produced no great effect.

Is it true that we are short of priests ? Are all those we already have employed to the best advantage ? Let us read again the decision taken by the apostles when they ordained deacons to take their place in their material ministry (Acts vi. 2–4); let us meditate upon it and it may be that our missionary apostolate will gain thereby.

And then let us look again at Urundi-Ruanda which, out of a population of three million (about the same as Paris), can claim five hundred and fifty-eight thousand eight hundred and thirty-eight Christians and one hundred and fifty-six thousand and sixty-nine catechumens. Could we say that in our capital there is an equal number of " real " Christians? Yet over there they have only one hundred and eighteen missionaries and forty-five native priests to carry out their work of the apostolate. Here we have not a success like theirs—on the contrary we are losing ground; and our priests *are ten times as numerous*. Does not this fact indicate that it is less a question of numbers than a question of methods?

Let us carry this instructive comparison a little further.

In one vicariate a tribe with a population of one hundred and fifty thousand has sixteen priests working in five mission areas: the Christians number twenty-five thousand: in Paris in the XVIIIth arrondissement the three parishes of Notre Dame de Clignancourt, Sainte Geneviève des Grandes Carrières and Sainte Hélène add up to the same total of population. Twenty-three priests are working in this tough area and there are only in the Paris arrondissement a tenth of the number of Christians that the missionary vicariate can boast.

In Dissin there are six thousand Christians out of forty thousand and only three priests; in St. Bernard de la Chapelle (still in the XVIIIth arrondissement) there are five priests, forty-one thousand inhabitants and a far smaller number of Christians.

It would be easy to go on endlessly; let us say once more: it is less a question of the number of the clergy than of the methods they employ.

The pivot of the missionary apostolate is the lay catechist. In Urundi-Ruanda there are two thousand and seventy-two men and one hundred and twenty-three women catechists. In Uganda one hundred and ten priests are helped by eight hundred and seventy-nine men and one hundred and forty-five women. The great number of these lay militants is of enormous interest: specially dedicated as " propagandists ", they are something unknown at home.

Out in the missions they have thought the problem through and have met it by methods both well adapted and flexible.

Why cannot we imitate these missionaries in far-off lands? The difficulties of the workman are facing us; the winning of the proletariat is an agonising problem demanding bold, energetic, perhaps startling measures, changes, it may be, in our whole set-up. At least do not let us shirk it by putting forward unreal excuses.

Need for Communities of a Natural Growth

NEW communities are springing up on all sides; we are witnesses of their birth, and we greet them with joy.

It is our second task to enter into each one of the actual worlds of which contemporary life is made up, and the basic means of doing this appears to be to ensure a powerful and dynamic Christian leaven in the very midst of these little communities.

It seems necessary to press this point again and again: Christian communities must be formed in all existent communities. This is the pivot on which the whole problem of urban missions turns: for four-fifths of the populace cannot practise as Christians excepting in and through these communities, nay, can hardly live a human life except in community. Their personalities are not strong enough for them to stand alone: they must lean on others: they require help. This help may come from a community foreign to their own, but on which little by little they centralise their lives. But this, as we have seen, is likely to occur only with a chosen few; the mass do not move out of their own world; the picked few, in abandoning it, leave it weaker and poorer.

Our efforts to help must consist of a double action on the proletarian masses.

There must first be an effort to make of the workers' world in general—of the entire modern world, which weighs so heavily on the individual—a more christianising, or at least a less de-christianising influence. This we may attempt in a twofold manner:

(*a*) By a slow transformation of all those things in modern life which make these influences concrete and overpowering— e.g. the cinema, the Press, the radio. A long, slow job; but, done thoroughly, it will be lasting.

(*b*) By working on that public opinion which in every society dictates the ideas of the moment. The anonymous masses are guided by *waves* of public opinion, and, do what we will, the proletariat will long consist of anonymous masses.

Only our second effort will solidify this work and make it lasting; it alone will attack the deep seat of evil: working towards the re-creation of those natural basic communities which are humanly necessary. For a community is other than a crowd. A community creates within itself a core of goodness. Anonymous crowds, disorganised individuals, are led by sheer numbers or by the worst elements among them. Communities tend by their nature to accept the influence of their best men and to rise thereby.

In a true community the highest natural elements find positions of influence and functions worthy of them without having to leave their own class in order to rise. A crowd of followers developed by a more human atmosphere can be helped to become an élite, and other followers in turn take their line from these. This social law seems evidenced by experience of life and by the facts cited in this book. There are modern thinkers (such as Thibon in his *Retour au Réel*) who believe that it is of the very nature of things.

Was it not anyhow the method chosen and forecast by Jesus Christ for the sanctification of His followers?

The religious community should be first a human community, real of its very nature. If it becomes the Christian nucleus of another true community its light will shine brightly and will attract many souls.

Such is the country parish: a Christian nucleus, with a semi-Christian borderland, set within the community of the village. Such were once our urban parishes in the great cities; such are still those in the small towns.

A Christian Community inside a Human Community

Christian soldiers in barracks sometimes form such a community. But suppose that in a garrison town Christians were brought together from ten different regiments or barracks, were distributed alphabetically in a dozen communities. They might become very fervent, they might produce saints, but they would not be a radiating force in each community because they would not correspond with the community. You would have strong conquering Christian personalities helping some of their brethren, but seen from inside the barracks they would have rather an air of assertive individualism.

Individuals may have influence; the community has a power of conquest that wins for itself more and more members.

It is noteworthy how relatively easy the Christian triumph becomes even in a fully pagan country once a small community of Christians has been built up within a natural human community which can look at it, judge of it, admire it. This was the case in the Stalags and the Oflags and resulted in an apostolate surprisingly successful under the circumstances whenever it was oriented in a missionary direction.

So, too, in country parishes, where it seems always possible if one perseveres (country people react slowly) to form, by the right methods, a certain nucleus, unless there is some obstacle preventing fusion among the Christians. For, it can never be repeated too often, individual fine personalities will not influence the masses. If in a factory ten Catholics are working who all live in different parishes, going to Mass, Confession and Communion at their parish churches, but spending all their working and leisure hours among their comrades in the factory, clearly that factory, its work, its amusements, its comradeship make up their true community. Suppose each one tries to do the work of an apostle among those nearest to him, but they meet seldom and briefly, they may decide perhaps on lines of action, but they will not become a community. And if there is no community, the less earnest are apt to become discouraged and fall away; certainly they will not win over the crowd they work among. They cannot become a mission. What is lacking is a priest to help them in creating a true, dynamic community belonging to, radiating in, that particular factory, becoming part of its life.

The first task of a really popular Catholic mission to the people must be that of discovering all the existent human communities and of forming in each one of them a Christian nucleus which, with the help of a priest, will itself become a light-bearing community.

The Fundamental Cause of De-christianisation

The great disaster of the last century was the extinction of all those basic communities which help men to develop. Uprooted, lost in a nameless crowd, a man becomes simply an individual. To be a person he must experience that development which various groupings produce in various degrees.

To re-make these forms of common life, to make their influence a Christian influence, to create within each one a little Christianising world, would be to swim against the current of our present paganism. It is because we have not done so sooner that paganism has overwhelmed us.

People often point to the pitiable lot of the worker around 1830. The gross abuses of that time accelerated the loss of faith, strengthened the paganism of today and paved the way for that Communism which has done so much harm: on their authors rests a heavy responsibility for our ills. But that they are not the only cause becomes clear when we reflect that, generally speaking, the section of the population that first came into the cities, lived the heroisms and experienced the injustices of industrial life (in the north for instance), have, in spite of it all, remained more Christian. It is those who came later from the country into towns where working conditions had become moderately good (Gennevilliers, Montreuil, etc., towns whose growth dates from after the war of 1914) who are far and away the most pagan.

The chief cause of the loss of Christianity among the proletariat, the cause from which spring all the others, is the *uprooting* of these new city-dwellers. They have lost the powerful support of their village communities and have found in the cities no basic communities to replace them.

And so they have not been able even to live a really human life, for the absolutely indispensable first elements of social existence are lacking. Everything is de-spiritualised, everything is de-personalised. Their Christianity had been a community life, and with all their other forms of community life it, too, had been swept away. Only exceptionally strong characters could develop at all in such surroundings.

But the thing might be made to work the other way. The Christian conquest is more arduous among workmen of a higher level, closer to the middle classes, very individualistic and aware of themselves, than in the entirely proletarian districts in which there always remains some degree of community life.

I am inclined to think that the gathering in of a handful of fine personalities is easier on the higher level, but mass conversion easier among the real proletariat. It is indeed noteworthy how many communities have of late sprung up in their midst and continue to do so at an ever increasing pace. The best judges estimate that this flowering of communal life is a real beginning of something, though it has yet far to go.

It would seem that our job is to help the State—by personal activity and by putting pressure on institutional groups—in re-creating those communities which are indispensable if family life is once again to become really human and thus really Christian. Look closely and you will see that most proletarians belong to some community—whether of their district, their working life or their free time. Until there exists something more lasting, let us fall in with the life of these transitory groups. It would seem impossible to raise, to educate, to make moral and Christian that shapeless element among the masses who live remote from any community life and who have no one to aid them. But this state of things can hardly be permanent in the world of today. The workers tend towards communal life. Yet it seems, too, that in their actual scheme of living each person or each family actually forms a part of only one community which is the centre of his life and the area inside which he is helped by others to live. This theory is confirmed by the facts. A Christian militant who is a real leader is so only in the community on which his life is centred. It is his district, *or* his factory, *or* some particular youth movement, *or* some free-time group, but never all these together.

When then the religious problem comes before our proletarians it comes at that angle of their life on which their interests are centred (social questions perhaps or healthy employment of spare time, ideal of personal living or love), but not all together.

Jean and Lucienne, Paul and Odette, and many others seeking to fathom the depth of their mutual love, found themselves up against the problem of religion, while at least one young woman became a Christian at the moment when motherhood introduced her to a woman's fullest life.

A young group made the discovery when searching for a solution of the social problems of our age, while another group camping out on a holiday found that in the tranquillity of nature they began to realise God's presence and to feel their own need for religion.

One sporting team learnt that to remain fully men they must balance the cult of the body by something else.

And many of the young have been won by the very fashion of their youth. Like all youth, they were seekers—seekers after an ideal worthy of their young manhood which they could find nowhere else.

Any of these angles will do for the asking of the question. When Christianity comes, bringing with it the answer, it will gradually take possession of the whole of life.

Christian Communities All Around Us

In the world of labour itself we may, as we have seen, find many a true community not spread over a whole vast combine, but in a particular workshop, the employees of certain offices, some special team. Imperfect as they are, these are the communities that get most deeply down into the lives of the workers. It is through them that Communism got in among the masses with a speed and to a depth from which we have not yet recovered.

The Charte du Travail tends to strengthen and to multiply these communities. Noting that the proletariat can only be educated and elevated in groups, and despairing of the erection in the big cities of local communities small enough (i.e. groupings of a few hundreds) to become these basic communities, the Charte endeavours to build them up on a professional basis. It plans later to transfer on to the same basis most works of popular education and some spheres of holiday arrangements. The Charte may fail, but in any case the group tendency remains.

Very fertile if uncertain ground for the discovery in the post-war period of groups that could be christianised is the use of free time. In the fundamentally weakened state of public health doctors fear the worst unless a great effort is made by the authorities for the inhabitants of big cities to get a great deal of open-air life. These authorities are in fact preparing such a programme ahead of everything else and it will be one of startling dimensions. It is also probable that industry, once more over-equipped for reconstruction, will quickly reach an unemployment period that enforces leisure hours.

Dwellers in big cities will be able, will be invited, indeed it may be an understatement to say will be " induced ", to spend their Sundays and part or the whole of their Saturdays in the country.

It would be jumping too far forward to make detailed plans in this matter, but it would surely be lacking in prudence not to look ahead. Here is a field for the work of Christian organisations and missions the magnitude of which is hard to imagine.

Then, too, there are local communities of all sorts and kinds, whether set up officially or simply an existing fact, of which there are so many in popular districts. Again there are quasi-natural communities which have never been set up as such: typical of these are the wives of our prisoners. One would only have to bring them together and, behold, a community would be born. These, too, should be won over by a centre of Christians at the heart of them.

In every mass of dough we must insert the leaven: in every group a smaller group organised towards conquest. It is said that we must " multiply parishes " if we are to re-christianise. Yes, multiply by all means those parishes that have become too big to be real communities, but this remains an internal problem of Catholicism; a mission is something that reaches out beyond.

One Paris arrondissement of two hundred and eighty-five thousand inhabitants is served by seven parishes: Lille and its suburbs for a practically equivalent population has seventy, and these are still too vast to form real communities. In point of fact there exist dioceses (Calvados for instance) the population of which is smaller and which have two hundred and fifty, four hundred and even eight hundred parishes.

A mission reaches further, multiplies a thousandfold more;
A Christian centre in this shop;
Another in that office;
A Christian kernel among those hikers;
Another in that group of actors;
In that huge family boarding house the leaven has been kneaded in;

And in that great block of workman's flats;

Leaven in that professional school;

Leaven in that evening class of five hundred youths;

Leaven among the allotment workers;

Leaven among that group of cinema actors;

Leaven among that neighbourhood team, among the heads of families of the district, in that syndicate, in that committee for social work;

Leaven among the association of doorkeepers of the VIIth arrondissement, among the artists of Montmartre, among the shopgirls of the Boulevard or of the Place du Louvre;

Christian action everywhere corresponding with life as it is being lived, moulded upon its shapes, built up with a missionary outlook, made to a missionary design.

IT WOULD be disastrous to think that the establishment of missions relieves the rest of the Church from its duty to win the world. Every individual Christian, every group, is obliged to the utmost extent possible to help their wandering brothers to find the way back. The " elder brothers " must not only put away all narrowness and jealousy, but must hold out their arms to the prodigals.

This depends supremely on our conception of what being a Christian means. Here is the great problem.

Vocation of the Christian

In our view a Christian is not merely one who enjoys the advantages and the training which religion brings with it, who lives his own life in touch with God, but one who (in greater or less degree according to his degree of holiness) gives himself to a Cause.

What is the essence of our Christianity: what is the end we are proposing for all these means: what is our role as priests?

The first commandment, in which is contained all the law and the prophets, which Christ repeated tirelessly, which the apostles loved to recall, is that of *charity*, not a charity simply of feeling, but a charity of action, charity worked out not without struggle and effort. All our tasks are opportunities for the practice of this charity which is *the* great Law.

The mission of each one of us, our share in the coming of God's kingdom, is to offer to God and man that degree of love which is ours to give.

And as the author of the Law is the author of nature, nature itself will give us a thousand opportunities to exercise our love of God and of our neighbour.

Love of God. We are poor feeble men, prone to sin, always needy, always hungry for something, always uneasy about the future. All this should make easy for us the exercise of a thousand forms of love of God, ranging from petition to self-abandonment.

Love of our brethren. Man is essentially social. He needs his brother men and he is indispensable to them.

The family will first give him many daily opportunities to practise that love which is its very basis. Everything in the family exists for mutual love, and the Christian will find thousands of duties of love in daily family life.

Work represents another form of human solidarity and gives us many an opportunity of practising charity. Even the work itself is a contribution to human happiness, and the circumstances in which it is carried on (especially in our age) usually involve a high degree of collaboration and mutual dependence.

Other social surroundings offer many occasions for the practical exercise of Christianity: our native land, our own town or countryside, those who live near by, those who share our amusements, etc. etc. Every Christian in every community has a mission of his own, a mission of charity. Herein lies his function, his office, his job, his vocation. A job, a vocation not self-chosen but laid upon him by providential circumstances, that is to say by God Himself. This vocation is his primary function, to be put ahead of any other act of devotion self-chosen or more to his taste. In this lies the criterion of a Christian civilisation.

Already half Christian are a mother who brings up her children with a great deal of love, a workman who is obliging with his comrades, or, still better, who puts his whole heart into his job. That girl is a Christian who carries out her duties of girlhood in a spirit of charity and joyfulness, Christian that poor man who shares the bread he has begged with one poorer than himself.

The Christian's Twofold Duty

All this makes the apostolate of the Christian laity sufficiently clear. We have a double function on earth: to let the light shine in our personal lives and to radiate also as members of society. It follows that we have two functions as Christians, two duties of the apostolate. The first is shown in the parable of the talents (social life).

We must serve God by making Him radiate through our personal lives, by being in some way or other one of those saints who elevate their surroundings, who help their brethren to rise. This apostolate belongs essentially to one's own milieu, and the more closely one is identified with that milieu the more efficacious is it.

But the more one belongs to a particular milieu the further one is away from all the others.

This personal apostolate is essentially Catholic Action. " The workers will become the apostles of the workers, " said Pius XI, and in the same way doctors and social workers will be the apostles of doctors and social workers.

But each of us has also a social *function*, a job to carry out in the world, or, more accurately speaking, two: one in the scheme of the family, another in that of professional life. The relative importance of these two varies considerably according to the importance of the professional function. Pasteur's family went for very little, while in the life of a normal woman the family function holds much the largest place.

These functions bring with them a duty of apostolate: to put at Christ's service our social influence: our duty as priest, as doctor, as officer, as officer's wife, as mother of a family; to carry out all these vocations as Christians.

This duty of apostolate is different from the personal apostolate of Catholic Action. It even in some respects cuts across it.

A doctor devoting himself wholeheartedly to his vocation as a Christian doctor turns away perhaps from his fellow practitioners whom he considers too commercial; he disapproves of them openly; he judges them severely. He has not enough love of his own world to be able to influence it. His two functions are not rightly balanced.

May it not be that priests have devoted themselves so exclusively to the second (their function as priests) that they have sometimes forgotten the first—brotherly help, life in community ?

These are among the many examples that might be given of a possible rivalry between the two ways in which we have to work for the coming of God's Kingdom.

The Christian's concern must be twofold:

(1) To bring his share of good into the society in which he lives.

(2) To contribute to the life of God in his brethren through the function that is his in the City.

This twofold effort tends towards the one end: he must live his Christianity in the whole of his life so as to help others to live it also.

The Mission of the Priest

We can now perhaps delimit accurately the scope of the priest's christianising action, his function as pastor or as missionary. To make Christians, *real* Christians, means to make every individual conscious of his duty of charity towards God and his brethren and then to help him by prayer, the sacraments—in one word by life in a Christian community— to exploit the possibilities to the full of his life as a Christian.

The task of the clergy is to make clear to each one this twofold vocation of everyday and all day long and help him to carry it out.

THIS book has been written in an attempt to get at the truth without bias. It is incomplete: it does not deal with all the problems that present themselves to the Christians of our age. The fact that some of these are omitted does not mean that we think them unimportant. There is, for instance, the problem of "this-world" action—of the rebuilding of "the City" on new principles. For we can have no illusions about its present foundations. The final aim of our work is not the conversion but the extinction of the proletariat, but that is a task that must be undertaken by human society—by the City— as a whole. We have not only to bring the masses to Christ, we have to make them into something that is no longer a shape-less mass.

Our world of today is not human; it is sick; it is funda-mentally corrupt. It is not certain that under present con-ditions we can bring the masses as a whole to church. (I don't say bring them *back*—for the Church has never possessed them since they first began to exist, say from 1830 to 1880.)

This unhealthy civilisation is exceptionally resistant to the Gospel. First because liberal capitalism and the exclusive reign of profit have deeply corrupted morals and institutions.

Mammon is the ruler of this world.

And again in the rush towards individual liberty and per-sonality which characterises the modern world the value of communities has been overlooked, and they have been destroyed as part of a frantic effort to change the world over. The world has, in fact, been organised as though every man were strong enough to live in isolation. The law of humanity has been forgotten: leaders who draw after them those more apt to follow, assisted by basic shapes of life. The world today starts where it should end. It desires for every man complete liberty, a strong personality. The idea is fine even if it savours of Utopia. Life might be called upon to help to bring it about, but the world has been organised as though it were there already.

Hence the masses are almost as impenetrable to culture as to religion.

But this is not a reason either for sitting still or for bending all our efforts on changing our civilisation.

The first Christians did not begin by destroying slavery, but they made Christians of the best of the slaves despite their state of slavery. So, too, we can begin by establishing Christian groups within every community, even the most proletarian. This book has shown how far we are from having done so. But it has also shown that in fact, as a matter of experience, aside from any intellectual theory, a great number of adult pagans, a still larger number of young ones, are waiting for the Faith, are crying out for it. To offer them a strong, youthful Christianity is to give to the world that is now being built the only foundations on which the building can be solid.

But let these masses be " de-proletarianised " while no Christian leaven has begun to work in their midst and they will adopt some form of pagan culture and become harder to convert than if they had no culture at all. There are striking instances of this in most of the districts where the workers have raised themselves from a human point of view.

Side by side with our religious effort there is an immense social and political work to be done; indeed it is only in a world whose very structure is in the course of political and social renewal that the re-christianisation of the masses can be *completed*. This renewal is the task of the City whose job it is to achieve that temporal well-being which facilitates the spiritual development of the nations and sometimes actually conditions that of the masses.

It must be admitted that up to the present the City has taken no interest in the spiritual development of the masses, has taken too little interest in their material development and is only now beginning to diagnose the evils of their inhuman existence. The Church is concerned with temporal affairs only by the way and only for eternal ends, "ratione aeternitatis". But Christian principles alone can bring about a real renewal. Faced by the deficiencies of the earthly City, its incapacity, its incompetence, the Church has historically over and over again supplemented the task of the State. But today the State is of age and will no longer agree to have its deficiencies supplied from outside.

The Church must still assist the State. But to examine the question of this most necessary help is outside the scope of this book.

And, anyhow, all efforts at renewal, even those based on Christian principles, will fail, unless at the same time there is a great and powerful Christian revival among the masses.

We do not say

Politics first,

Nor normality first,

Nor social effort first.

For a great upsurging of a young, powerful Christianity must be sustained by all these efforts simultaneously.

The world cannot be saved without Christ and His grace. All this political and social renewal is not Christianity: it is, let it be repeated, in the domain of the City. It will, however, clear away the difficulties, the barriers that impede the Christian revival. And it can only be achieved in the atmosphere of a youthful Church. Whatever their founders intend, all institutions are deeply stamped in their very being by the spirit of their members as a whole.

"Politics first" takes us into a vicious circle just as "an exclusively spiritual Christianity" does. We need both, each doing its part. And the first is an essentially lay work.

In their ardour to rebuild the City some people seem to become over-concentrated on questions of statecraft. No doubt skill in this may gain temporary advantages for us, and an influence on our institutions of imposing appearance, but these successes would soon be turned against us if it was discovered that practising Christians were only a tiny minority.

The real influence of the Church, the influence Christ taught her to gain, the influence exercised by the apostles is surely that of a deep Christian penetration into a multitude of souls whose light shines through their entire existence. It is very certain that the Church will not win back the proletariat unless she brings to an end the " greatest scandal of the nineteenth century ". We may execute successful manœuvres, but we shall have no troops on the battlefield.

Only a *mystique* can stand against a *mystique* : not reasonings, or lamentations, or tactical positions utterly disproportionate to this great matter. Against a dynamic vision only a more dynamic can succeed. The whole proletariat of France will offer all its millions of men and women, the wealth of its young energies, to the *mystique* which is preached to them first, which answers best to the deepest cry of their souls, which appears to them the freshest and most dynamic.

We must listen to the call of Pius XII in his Christmas message of 1942; we must try to understand at long last the serious, nay agonising, problem of the workers' world. May the cry that arises from its depths move our hearts, a cry " for justice and brotherhood in the world of a just God ".

If we do not set missions on foot for our proletarians who lack religion and culture, others will do it. Soon they will have a culture and a religion, too. Please God that religion may not be too unlike the religion of Christ.

PART III

THE BREAD IS RISING

To a friend who remonstrated with him for destroying his health by overwork and lack of care, Abbé Godin said, " I have the right to shorten my life a little if the work to be done is of vital urgency." But it was after another fashion that God had accepted his total offering, and the very suddenness of his going had made his life and his book stand out uniquely. My own copy is an old one: already eighty thousand had been sold, and year by year the sale mounts. It has been followed by such a multitude of other books, many largely inspired by it, that it is hard to keep track of the literature produced by the now vitally missionary Church of France. A French priest, himself editor of a magazine, told me the other day that everything was moving so fast he found himself constantly out of date. The news is stop press. And it suffers from this very fact. For it is unimportant but startling facts that make the headlines: there are priests wearing lay clothes and working in factories: some Bishop has given permission for Mass to be said in the evening, or facing the congregation.

Anyone who has seen a French priest in a soutane riding a woman's bicycle can understand that lay clothes would hold a strong appeal for the younger clergy. But in the movement it is generally treated as a merely practical question; in the same group a priest going to a factory may wear lay clothes, one staying at home his soutane or his habit. And these minor matters are treated in complete deference to authority. Abbé Hollande the superior sees all the priests of the Mission de Paris weekly, he reports to Cardinal Suhard monthly and goes to Rome frequently. This is typical of the spirit of the movement. Indeed, in one book a warning note is sounded about the use of any unusual methods without serious reasons—they

" are a public danger with men who find it easier to put on an act than to think.

" Undisciplined pupils produce progressively stricter rules in a college.

" Imprudent priests who apply the best formulas without discernment bring about a multiplication, which the Bishops themselves often regret, of canonical prohibitions to right and left. . . .

" There is only one apostolate, and that is to put a soul in touch with God. . . . God's work calls for more subtlety on the part of the apostle. The salvation of souls is not effected by quasi mechanical proceedings. To put a soul in touch with God is not a material task but a kind of childbirth."

It was in this spirit that the head of the French Church had himself addressed the gathering at Lisieux. It is impossible to estimate the greatness of Cardinal Suhard's share in the transformation of the French scene that we witness today. Here are the directives given by him on the 13th and 14th of January, 1944, to the Mission de Paris.

" Today a great thing is happening at Lisieux: so thanks to God, through St. Thérèse, for both the Mission de France and the Mission de Paris.

" Souls are on the move, there is a general stirring: it is realised that our country will rise again only when it is a Christian nation, *with a missionary soul*.

" To that end, the Mission de France and the Mission de Paris are *powerful ideas*.

" 1. We must realise that the Mission de Paris is *a great enterprise*. The work of the Mission is the specific work of Christ. He came to save souls, He came only for that.

" The masses are cut off from the Christian community, so the priest must have the missionary spirit. *We do not do the whole of our duty in attending to those who come to church: that would be apathy, a defect in the sense of pastorship.*

" 2. The bases of the Mission:

" First, the *Charity* of Christ;

" Then *Piety*, to show the *true face* of Christ (the Piety must be nourished on the Gospel);

" *Devotion* and the *total giving* of self. We must be prepared for checks, trials, contradictions, misunderstandings;

" *Prudence*—which does not exclude boldness—and great generosity;

" *Doctrine*—we must convince, instruct catechumens by giving them as much of the totality of doctrine as they can take;

" *Discipline*—this will be the *strength* of the group, and the way to avoid aberrations.

" 3. The position to be taken.

" You will have your position, once you have succeeded. Meanwhile

" (1) In relation to the Pagans: you must go in among them—hence *boldness*: but always remain *priests*;

" (2) In relation to existing Catholic societies: you must use them and be useful to them. In fact, it is from them that you will get the first missionaries. Hence sympathetic understanding and good relations.

" (3) In relation to the Parishes: They exist and the Mission must complement them (*doit les compléter*). Hence play fair with the Parish Priests (*droiture et loyauté avec MM. les Curés*)."

On January 14 His Eminence added:

" The direct object of the Mission de Paris is to convert the pagans. Its indirect object, *to show the Christian Community that it has to take a new attitude*: a shock has to be given. Much has been done in this last fifteen years, especially with Catholic Action; we must go further and *it is for the Mission to show the direction*. Hence: Emphasis on Truthfulness, Modesty, Humility and Respect for all good that is being done.

" Charity towards fellow-workers.

" Clear statement to the Christian Community that it may grasp that upon it lies the duty of making conversions. Set up in the souls of Christians a *salutary uneasiness*.

" 4. How the Mission is to proceed.

" *Think out a method:* then experiments, corrections, necessary adaptations; to succeed, account must be taken of each man's *personal qualities*: each must form himself, reform himself. You must have *tenacity of effort*: the Mission is a long-term enterprise. The Missionary must be upheld by his love of Christ and his love of the Church."

" Unless the grain of wheat falling into the ground die, itself remaineth alone." How often had Henri Godin quoted those words: how deeply realised that all great works must begin in sacrifice, that to get from the human to the divine we must pass through Calvary. The story of the first weeks after his death as his friends tell it is like the morrow of the crucifixion : the glow that is upon them today like the dawn of Pentecost.

There is nothing spectacular about the Mission de Paris. It does not work through organisations human or divine, it is not itself much organised, it does not try to train leaders or to work specially on those who are naturally great; it is just the leaven in the dough of human life; it is the Spirit blowing where it listeth, and if you go out into that air you find it is blowing very powerfully.

But the beginning was anguish. At the first meeting of the Mission very few were present and those chiefly layfolk. One priest, close friend of Henri Godin's, had broken down completely. All were overwhelmed by the burden of responsibility, by losing a greatly loved leader who had not even left them a plan. I am sure that Godin was determined never to be a Holy Founder—never to let the forms established by him prevent the changes that time should bring, the natural evolution of a living organism, never to let his followers say, " Our Holy Rule forbids——"

Of all who were suffering, his mother came first. To Doctor Tremolière she wrote:

"My poor Abbé was my only reason for living, my sole support. I still have another son, equally good and kind, but a married son can never be what he was to me. . . . I am sometimes amazed at having survived this shock; I would rather not have survived it.

"I shall offer to God for you all, Priests and Laymen of the Mission de Paris, my sufferings and my loneliness, so that I may not be entirely useless in this world since I must stay here still."

But it was in keeping with this story, lived in the depth of human life, that she did not content herself only with prayer and suffering. A friend of the Mission presently offering a house near Orléans for a rest home for workers, this old lady of eighty left her home in the Jura and went with her married son and his wife to look after it. French country folk do not move easily: it was to leave the home, the friends, the associations of a long lifetime. And the task was a herculean one. The German army had occupied and gutted the house; little was left but the walls, and in the last four years about a million francs from the accumulated royalties of Godin's books (which he rarely touched) have gone into repairs.

Madame Godin is still alive, but it is now her son and daughter-in-law who look after the house. For, after a most painful illness, both her legs have been amputated. She still offers her sufferings and her solitude for the work of her son.[1]

That son one seems to see and hear as one meets the children of his work, so vivid is his presence to them still.

Roger Beaunez told me how he had been bidden to the discussions at Lisieux and how his fiancée had grumbled a little at losing him for Christmas. Abbé Godin had written, " *There must be many sacrifices for the redemption of the masses:* sacrifices of priests, and sacrifices also of the Christian people." Whereupon she was sorry she had complained and told him so. " Be

---

[1] She died while this book was in the press.

at peace," he answered; " be happy and do not get worried because you are sometimes simply ' human '. The only people who are otherwise are saints ready to be canonised and hypocrites who pretend not to be. I bless you with all my heart."

And now Roger is alone with two adorable little girls. For his wife died when the second was born. Owing to her health the doctor had feared, had wanted to take the child away months before. " But my wife wouldn't let him. It would have been a medical abortion. We knew all those months that she would die." And he went on to note that of the layfolk engaged in the Mission four of the women had lost their husbands before the war came to an end. He, too, struck the note: we must suffer; we must sacrifice for the work. He is bringing up his children " en pleine vie ". The two-and-a-half-year-old has already been hitch-hiking with her father through the night, has learnt to wake up readily, to fall asleep again. I wonder what the child's grandmother with whom they live thinks of his educational methods! " Il ne faut pas couver les enfants."

Before I went to Paris I had thought of the Mission as mainly clerical, but through Père Chenu, O.P., and Doctor Tremolière I came to know how very much of it is the radiation of the Jeunes Foyers. At the réco of Montreuil Père Chenu had said Mass for the layfolk who were *leaders* of groups in that area alone: forty-eight were present.

As we have seen, the absence of organisation by no means meant the lack of general lines that should guide the Mission in its early steps. Among the Lisieux outlines there is quite a bit about these little groups. A priest, it is said, may well be the personal head of two or three and the chaplain of another three, the heads of which are layfolk. The words " militant " or *dirigeant* are not to be used, but rather " Christian " and " Head of a Christian Community ". (I wish we had one English word for Chrétienté.)

The community spirit must be maintained in every way; mutual services, mutual enjoyment, above all prayer together.

The great feasts of the Church should be again brought into prominence; there must be some degree of community prayer. This is, of course, achieved supremely by Mass in a home—but something there must be—if it is only a minute's silence the purpose of which has been first explained.

As to private prayer and meditation, the point was made that the modern industrial age makes the old daily rhythm of spiritual life extremely difficult. Where daily periods of quiet are quasi-impossible it was suggested that the spiritual life, like the life of labour, be geared to a weekly rhythm centring on the weekend the heart of which is Sunday.

To keep up its fervour it is wiser that a group should not exceed thirty in number. They will have among them " catechumens " (or enquirers), who may even remain so for two or three years.

At periodical meetings there should be an examination of what influence the group is producing and the judgement, from a Christian point of view, of the happenings in their natural communities of daily life.

They should be taught *how* to serve their neighbours rather than have specific services planned out for them.

Each group should meet weekly or fortnightly, and there should be occasional meetings of the heads, especially with a view to each one realising his own littleness by meeting those who are his equals or his superiors in self-devotion. For leadership by itself is apt to go to the weak human head.

Montreuil is the area where the Mission is strongest and also most widely scattered, and it is felt by many that Abbé Depierre is the closest to Abbé Godin in his almost prophetical outlook on the Christian future of the proletariat.

He has started in the area two working teams to give employment in hard times. One group breeds rats and mice for the laboratories, another goes out into the country and cuts wood, which is brought into Paris and sold there. Others concern themselves with finding lodgings for the homeless. Then, too, a group of young men go outside Paris and work on the land a good part of the year. Another rest-house has been started by the Montreuil section of the Mission—and Doctor Tremolière told me, with smiles, of the contrast between the running of this and of the Godin house. Monsieur Godin is a practical peasant. " For him two sous are two sous. If you are very poor you don't pay at all, but if you have the two sous you must pay them." Then, too, punctuality is insisted on and order, rules must be kept: " You have no right to tear the sheets." " You have no right to come in at three if lunch is at twelve." But Abbé Depierre is a visionary, and in his vision the community is supreme: no rules, no order; the community is to decide. The result, says the doctor, is that the Mission is always having to produce cash. " So at last we said to him, ' Well, if the community is to run the place the community must find the money.' He wasn't pleased. But," concluded the doctor, " the community has managed to find most of it."

It would, of course, be impossible to reduce to these activities, to shut up in a formula, even the temporal works of the lay groups. " Generous families," says Abbé Depierre, " become transformed into the Churches of their neighbourhood, mothers of children become ' maman ' to their whole street."

Literally churches: for it is in these houses that Mass is said of an evening for the workers. They gather round a table and the priest stands facing them. At the Memento of the living and of the dead he asks them for whom they want prayers: we prayed one night I was there for a sick child, for a family that lacked bread, and then for all who toiled and were heavily burdened. As the Collect literally means a gathering by the priest of his people's prayers, so now these petitions are gathered into the Great Action which this little group is learning to understand. All have permission to go to Communion without preliminary fast; almost all do go. And by way of *Ite Missa est*, the priest says to them at the end, " Allez, c'est votre mission." After Mass the " Mother " prepares supper for all who care to stay.

Each of these houses is a " living cell ", says Abbé Depierre, made up of those who desire to " engage themselves totally for the salvation of humanity ". Two doctors, the head of a factory, one scholar, came humbly to beseech him to let them become factory workers and " dwellers in our poor district so as to share better in the fate of the masses and throw all their cultural achievements into the salvation of all ".

One little story related by Père Loew, in his fascinating book *En Mission Prolétarienne*, tells more than volumes of the meaning of joining your life with the life of the proletariat—or perhaps here what is called the sub-proletariat. A boy of his acquaintance had lost his ration book. Almost unable to write, unapt at explaining his problems, with no time for queueing, he had relinquished all hope of getting another, when Father Loew took the matter in hand. After queueing for hours and filling in a multitude of forms, he returned with his prize. The boy's delighted parents begged him to dine with them and celebrate. They would not take no for an answer, and as they sat down to dinner the lad remarked, " You needn't be worried, Father, about eating our rations. I got all this out of garbage pails."

After the first mouthful, Father Loew comments, with plenty of pepper and salt it didn't taste too bad.

PURSUED by the Hound of Heaven, the poet uttered his fear, " Lest having Thee I might have naught beside." But exactly the opposite has happened. With the loss of God all the rest has been lost. " Can you tell me," said an atheist to a Catholic Evidence Guild speaker, dropping his voice from the loud confident blare in which he was wont to heckle, almost to a whisper, " whether a Catholic gets more out of life than an atheist? "

The poor pagans of today are not indeed atheists, but God is remote from them and it is not much they are getting out of life. In losing God they have lost human relationships: between employer and employee, between friend and friend, between brother and brother, between husband and wife. Trust is gone, and without trust nothing can cohere. Father Loew sees parental love as the only thing left to build on. Especially for young children this love has survived overcrowding, dirt, lice, want of food. A man still loves his little child.

The speaker answered the heckler: " Which gives most to life? "—and that is the answer given by the lives of these missionaries.

Father Loew stresses the fact that the idea of disinterested charity is lost by the modern world. Charity must be pure— even from appearing to be used for a spiritual apostolate. To the pagan the Church is still seen as a political organisation. A nun told Abbé Depierre how a workwoman coming to the convent after the victory of the Catholic party said, " Well, sister, I suppose you're all happy. It's a defeat for us workers, it's a victory for you." In the slums, worker and Communist are practically identical, and the Church means Conservative, bourgeois, exploiter. Our Lord's blessing is on *service* of the poor. Saint Vincent called them " our masters ". And just as he stopped the forced confessions of patients entering the hospital, so today the Mission will not have its charity made an instrument even of conversion. Remembering the painful story of " soupers " in Ireland, one quite sees their point.

Not that either priests or layfolk have much to give materially: their great gift is themselves. Generously as the lay cells make this gift, they are usually married people with personal responsibilities to their children and to one another which must of necessity come first. Almost from the beginning the Church has found ways for a more entire self-devotion to God and all men. Out of the movement is growing in France a new type of the religious life for women. Not actually called the religious life, it is suggestive in some respects of the deaconesses in the Early Church.

Assisting Father Loew, who has now taken over two parish churches in Marseilles, is a group of women who have what is called a Residence where they live and whence their work radiates. He notes that the governmental French social worker is discouraged from overdoing the personal element. But the Residence must be entirely personal. It must be a home: flowers on the tables, an air of welcome, time allowed for the release from tension, for the telling of the long involved tale. The residents themselves are urged to an intense spiritual life; daily Communion, meditation, reading of the Gospels; monthly days of prayer and study, three days every four months, one retreat a year. Father Loew's group is one of a number scattered through France. These teams are very small, sometimes only three women. They took part in a deeply interesting discussion this year, published as a supplement to *La Vie Spirituelle* on " Adaptations of Religious Life ". Members were present of orders as old as the Dominicans and as new as the Petites Soeurs de Jésus (Père de Foucauld), and the discussions are penetrated with zeal and enthusiasm. At the end the " lay " communities were asked to speak of their vocation. It was, they said, " to become wholly incarnated in a pagan world. Our missionary vocation is the essential: we exist for the pagans."

Community life brings with it " the virile element that prevents us from becoming old maids. . . . Through life we discover what may be asked of us. . . . We live on our wages, have nothing of our own, put everything at the service of others, money, even food, even clothes. Nothing belongs to us." Like religious they have a noviciate; in their missionary life they have a strong spiritual training. They study month by month some part of Scripture, " inserting it " in their lives. The thing shapes itself bit by bit. " It's a fairly adventurous life. . . . Where I am living there are anarchists, unmarried mothers. . . . I have been often asked who my lover is and whether I am going to have a baby. . . . But later when they know me better they don't say these things.

" One day talking about marriage one of them said, ' No, she isn't going to get married; no, it isn't that ' . . . There is something they begin to realise . . .

" It is a witness by being there, by being neighbourly, by charity. . . .

" Interiorly it means to go down very deep into the drama of the Incarnation and the Redemption . . . presence of Christ in this immoral, unbelieving world, search for Christ among them . . . they have in them Christian elements, Christian reactions of which they are unaware."

In calling themselves teams rather than communities these groups are following the missionary terminology of the Lisieux discussions.

The idea of a community is directly for the glory of God and the sanctification of its members—to be brought about by all sharing in the same spiritual exercises and all living exactly the same life. The word team, on the other hand, suggests a group directed towards a specific job, e.g. work on an aeroplane, in a factory or even to win a game.

" In our own case we shall use the word team because our reason for getting together is a job: the christianisation of the

Paris pagans. This implies our sanctification because our sanctification is a necessity for this work and because the work itself is sanctifying."

We are witnessing a new adaptation of the old ideals—but especially a new slant on the ideal of religious poverty. Of old, says Père Loew, the poor man was economical; he put by; he could save for old age. Today, especially among dockers and other casual labourers, this isn't possible. A docker holds his job from day to day, almost from hour to hour; he lives from day to day. Of old a convent was established on lines of economical poverty. But today the spirit of saving, of having something in hand, does not correspond with the rhythm of the neighbourhood poverty. A small convent, really poor, but also economical, shocked his dockers by the supplies they laid in. They were buying for a month or two ahead, which was a true economy especially for a number: but this a docker family, crowded into one room almost without cupboards and quite without the money to lay down all at once, could not realise. We must not, he concludes, have the poverty of the ant while we live among those who have the poverty of the grasshopper. Dwellers at the Residence have to earn their daily bread; in some cases they may allow their neighbours to pay them for their services (for instance for long periods of sick nursing), but they must share the rhythm of the lives around them. And this means that they must accept insecurity for themselves. " Il ne faut pas s'installer dans la vie."

And again the modern attitude should be considered in relation to what used to be the highest expression of religious poverty—the mendicant life. In the Christian Middle Ages a mendicant, having often given all he had to the poor, was felt to have a right to at least a minimum of support from his fellows. He was sometimes hungry as he went begging from door to door, but he was usually fed and almost always admired. Today it is different. A beggar is despised, he has " no right to live on the community ", " why doesn't he look for work ?" What is the answer? All our writers stress that they are still searching, are trying tentative experiments. But the teams of women, like the priest-workmen, find the answer for themselves in manual labour. Out of a team of three, two will go to the factory while one keeps house. They will usually take turns at this so that each may have the alternating period of (comparative) leisure and greater opportunity for prayer.

Women's work in factories is not in itself desirable, all this world is in flux and none knows what the future may bring. But, meanwhile, to be identified with the working masses they, too, work. While that minimum of security which Rome usually insists on as the basis of religious life they suggest may be found by them as by their proletarian sisters in earning a salary and having the wage-earner's right to the social securities of the modern State.

To Henri Godin, feeling his way, praying, suffering to bring to birth something greater than he knew, it had seemed that Saint Francis was the great model for a new experiment in poverty. And he chose a priest of deep historical learning, a Dominican, Père Chenu, to talk at Lisieux on the realisation in the modern world of what Saint Francis had done for the world of his own day. All the old orders, too, are in this new movement.

ABBÉ GODIN'S old bedroom in the Rue Ganneron is occupied by an educated layman who is now working in a factory where rags are sorted out for paper making. The flat itself and the one above it have become headquarters of the Mission where Abbé Hollande dwells: twenty priests are scattered through Paris in seven teams. Of these six are manual workers, three in factories, three on their own. Abbé Hollande asks that they should already have some pastoral experience, and they are sent for one year to the Seminary of the Mission de France at Lisieux to re-do their theology with a special bearing on their missionary work.

Before the war Père Chenu had sent one of his young Dominicans (as a novice) to work for a while in a factory.[1] At Lisieux the idea of a " stade ouvrier " had been approved for priests " providing they do not imagine it gives them a complete knowledge of the worker's life (they will not know what insecurity really means or the feeling that it is lifelong)." But the full conception of the priest-workman must be said to date from the war and to be almost entirely the result of the experiences of a considerable number of priests who had themselves been workmen—either in prison camps or with the deported labourers in Germany. It was one of these who, joining the Mission de Paris, begged Abbé Hollande to let him become wholly one with the workers in this fashion.

For some time Abbé Depierre worked as a shoemaker—until his " community " said to him, " You mustn't work any more, you are our priest, our father; we will look after you."

---

[1] Père Bouche, O.P. He is now one of the editors of *Masses Ouvrières* and a head chaplain of the J.O.C.

He is now in fact if not in name a parish priest. His parish consists of the proletarian and sub-proletarian masses scattered over a wide area.

The Mission de Paris is far from being the only source of priest-workmen. Père Perrin, S.J., author of *Priest-Workman in Germany*, is living now with another Jesuit in a miserable hole of a place—no water, no gas, no electricity—and working in a factory. Two Capuchins, Père André and Père Rogatien, have let me see the most moving record of their own experiences. It was only when their fellow-workers knew them *as men* that either group revealed the fact that they were priests. " What reaction was there? " Father Perrin was asked. " None whatever," he answered; " total indifference." Another priest was told he must never dare to come in his soutane or it would be torn off him. One of a Dominican group, Père Berger, analysed the usual series of steps. The workmen begin by thinking it a dodge on the part of the Church—a political move inspired by the Bishops or perhaps by the Pope. Then when they find that their priests do not mix in politics, that they are eager to do services to all around, that they will sacrifice themselves for the rest, the attitude becomes more sympathetic. Presently personal friendships form, workers will go home with the priest or will seek him out for practical advice. Père André and Père Rogatien have managed to get hold of a biggish wooden bungalow so that they are able to give a bed to anyone who needs it. (At one time they took care of a boy whose parents were quarrelling, until they got them to make it up.) The two work in different factories and by now each has become *our* priest, *our* curé. A third father lives with them to cook and clean for them and look after those who come for help during working hours.

The fact, Père Berger thinks, that the workman can *see* the priest facing the same difficulties as himself, balancing his budget (for normally they live on what they earn and draw no funds from their monasteries), establishes a link of very great value.

Even when it is possible, however, to have one man as housekeeper the problem of the priest-workman's health is quite a serious one. Of the teams with whom I established any contact nearly half were, or had been, resting under doctor's orders. For they are not accustomed to heavy manual labour for many hours a day. And when the labour is over comes the evening Mass and the priestly apostolate, often prolonged far into the night.

Father Loew describes touchingly the Mass of his fellow priest-workman in the house of a poor family. Mass, he says, is celebrated now in a home " in order to draw worshippers one day to the common home of all the faithful ". And he describes how his dockers reacted; how some brought flowers— " real flowers from a florist "; how gradually they learnt what Mass meant. One day he found a girl outside the door: " You're not coming to Mass today, Marinette? " " No, Father, I've had a quarrel with Juliette and I don't want to forgive her. So I can't say ' Forgive us our trespasses '." Two days later the belligerents were reconciled and came to pray together.

This Mass, too, was said in the evening. " More beautiful than the flowers were the careful but heavy genuflections of this priest who had been working all day at the docks and whose movements evidenced the weights he had been carrying. The mystery of the Redemption is taking place at the very spot where it is needed.

" Outside, the seven children of the Valès family are playing and when after our thanksgiving we meet in the court all hung with drying linen and old blankets being aired, life seems new to everyone.

" In the evening after supper, between visits from the neighbours, there is catechism and prayer which touches on all the little happenings of the day, the joys, the troubles of this district of workers."[1]

The priests who work in and near Paris meet often to pool their experiences and I have been privileged to see the

[1] *En Mission Prolétarienne, p.* 64.

unpublished records of one of these meetings. They discussed first whether it was best to dress " en civil " or to wear their habits. The Franciscans said the habit helped, by marking their priestly character, to bring them most fruitful contacts. Others thought that a deeper penetration was effected and even more remarkable apostolate resulted from the exterior identity with the worker. This, too, had been discussed at Lisieux. It would be worse, they said, for a priest to dress like a bourgeois than as a priest. Should he begin his mission dressed as a workman and then resume his cassock? No conclusion had been reached: a longer experience may decide the question or it may be left for the personal decision of each man. Rome has given full discretion in the matter to local authorities. Actually in the Mission de Paris of those I saw only Abbé Hollande was dressed as a priest.

Many of the priest-workmen are also Jocist chaplains. The young proletarians, said some, not only could not be integrated in parish sections, but for the most part were only interested in a section created by themselves. They did not want to join an existing section, even if proletarian. Père André had tried to affiliate about thirty boys to the J.O.C. and had found a dislike of any type of organisation whatever.

The question arose, should there be mixed groups of boys and girls? " Life is mixed," said one priest. On the whole the young were not inclined to be interested in the problems of the worker, or even in their own future, declared several. " We have to be especially on the watch against escapism in the young, which affects the area of their leisure hours and their religion."

Abbé Depierre is the only one of these priests who lives and works alone: all the rest are in teams. They were greatly moved and impressed by his thought that if there were several the workers spoke of them as " They ". But, living alone, he became so identified with his neighbours that they said " We ". All felt they must pray and think about this—but for the most part it was felt that for the spiritual life, mutual support, the apostolate itself, a team was preferable. For, after all, a priest can never be wholly identified with his flock. And it is not good even for the priest to be alone.

This question also had been discussed at Lisieux and the conclusions were headed, " Necessity for a priestly Community."

Living and working together calls for a two-fold attitude: (a) " to feel ourselves responsible for the spiritual ascent of our brothers in the team, to bear with their defects, to help them, to feel an obligation for the souls of our brothers; (b) to accept the fact that others have a part to play in our spiritual lives, to accept advice and some degree of supervision."

These communities too were to be called teams because community suggested the religious life and the Mission priests were and were to remain seculars. And for priests as for lay-men, " the spiritual life will often be lived on a weekly rather than a daily rhythm ". Spirituality must be more deeply inserted into daily life. " Draw profit from shocks in the intellectual order (by going at once to the very depth of the matter) and from shocks in the religious order (by moments of contact with God which give you back more than the shock cost you)."

Intensely interesting also is the report published in *L'Union* of a meeting between the heads of the various groups at which the principles that had emerged after some years' experience were analysed.

The Missions of Paris and of France were represented, and also the Petits Frères de Jésus (Père de Foucauld), the Jesuits, the Dominicans, the Capuchins and others. The conclusions underline both the importance of the movement and the dangers to be avoided.

Beginning with the reasons for undertaking such work, they divide them into two categories: the interior life of the priest, and the exterior apostolate. In either case they emphasise that it could only safely be done as the answer to a divine call. Those are unfit for it who desire it from " snobisme ", from the

wish to get away from a job they dislike, from class spirit.
" A positive vocation is needed and one that has had long
testing, a very pure vocation bearing the impress of the spirit
of Nazareth or of the Redemption, ready to break with
mechanical routine, to renounce success, to take up the cross.
Given this spirit, added to a clear call from God, it is certain
that ecclesiastical authority may not only permit but actually
' send ' a priest, that through him the Church itself shall be
incarnated in the working world."

The two reasons that may awaken this vocation are studied
in detail: if the priest goes for his own spiritual formation he
may for the time set aside the apostolate. He will live in the
spirit of Nazareth or of Christ on the Cross, developing in
himself the realisation of sin and suffering, living a life of prayer
in and through his work and gaining thereby " a more manly
spirit, the reactions of a man who is prepared for an apostolate
among adults. Those of middle-class education will get a very
healthy shock."

What has actually happened with Abbé Depierre is contemplated as a probability for the rest: that the day will come
for each man *when the community accepting him as their priest*
sets him free from all manual labour.

" And it may be that he will then become the parish priest
of a sort of personal parish made up of all those proletarians
who want to be Christians, but not like those other Christians
who in their eyes represent a class that has exploited and
enslaved them."

Among the problems faced in this discussion was the relation
of such a personal parish to the local church. In some localities
this is acute, in others it is already solved. The Capuchin
team are working in the Parish of the Sacred Heart, Petit
Colombes—a parish intensely missionary in its spirit and in
its structure. But, says Abbé Michonneau, in the book he has
written about it, however missionary a parish is it must *send*
out a mission into the areas it cannot reach. Such missions
are the " churches " in the factories, and with his authority the

Capuchin fathers even occasionally administer the Sacraments (baptism, penance, marriage) to their factory groups.

But it is on a second danger that the discussion dwells longest. There is in the working classes of today an upsurge of what can only be called "secular messianism". Can the priest take a part in this effort to change the shape of things, this battle on the political, economic and social front?

Their decision is that for the most part he ought not to do so—and the final phrase is striking. Sometimes it may be that through charity he gets involved; his passion for justice must remain, but he must not let it make him forget "the transcendent character of the priesthood, its mystery". He must never yield to hatred of anyone, be contaminated by "partisan passion".

"But," they conclude, "to keep this interior purity, whether with or without temporal entanglements, it is necessary to be strongly armed against desire for success, over-determination to be efficient. There must be a strong realisation of the Cross. The priest must be willing in advance to be rejected and crucified by the secular messianism when it has finally taken its shape."

The crowning means of apostolate in the vocation of priest-workman is also part of the second reason for which a man may be called: "the planting of the contemplative life and of the Church's mediation in the heart of working life".

This was the exact ideal of Charles de Foucauld, and it is not surprising that his sons should be among those who are carrying it out. On this, too, the group made points of the greatest interest. A priest who wants to carry it out for life must not, through a spirit of redemption, undertake work beyond his strength, but something to which he is physically equal. He must take part in the free-time occupations of the workman only in the measure suited to the priestly character. And although the silence enforced by the noise of machines may in many factories be positively favourable to contemplation, yet the priest must be very sure to reserve long periods at every week-end for prayer and spiritual refreshment.

Only prudent men, they concluded, men of judgment and men of prayer, must be chosen for this daring experiment, which is making of a missionary country a land of missionaries.

IV. THE OLD AND THE NEW

THE CLASH of ideas is constantly visible between the young Christianity bent on conquest that is inspiring so many today, and the old timid withdrawn attitude that allowed secularism to sweep over France. There is much of it still left, and Catholic Action often assails it vainly.

A typical story is that of a young schoolteacher whose letters have recently been published. Converted from unbelief to Catholicism, her life was spent in a village where she lived alone and had to handle the school unaided, where she became a marked woman by going to church, especially on a weekday. A big, cold house in bad repair: meals to get, cleaning to do, lessons to prepare. And then at night letters to her director which can only be called an orgy of introspection. She had passed her examinations brilliantly and had clearly a good mind: this is evidenced both by the books she read and the books he forbade her to read. It is evidenced by her affection for the upright, intellectual, unbelieving woman who had taught her and been her early inspiration. The director's own letters are not given, but the line is clear enough. One whose prime need was to get outside herself is turned inward. Her old teacher wanted her to read a book of Bergson's: the director forbade it. Nor might she read Tolstoy. She could have met her fellow-teachers on the weekly holiday in the neighbouring town, but was advised only to meet them monthly. She was taught to pray, and clearly she grew in prayer; she practised austerities; she was constantly sent home ill; she died of consumption, hoping to the last to be able to enter a Benedictine convent.

Truly, as Godin said, the convert from paganism is taken out of his world to leave it a little poorer instead of learning to win his world. The tragedy of this life is not her own tragedy: she loved God and did what she was told. But how can this be the authentic note of His religion who said, " Let your light shine before men ", and " I am come to cast fire upon earth and what will I except that it be kindled "?

Had this director been a missionary, could he have left the ninety-nine sheep in the desert while thus concentrating on the one who had got safely into the fold? Lost sheep do not commonly go round looking for the shepherd, and the shepherd seeking passionately for the lost multitude would not have the time for this long—I had almost written futile—correspondence. Contrast Abbé Godin's attitude to his young disciples as he goes out with them conquering and to conquer.

I asked the priest of an unusually vital parish in a proletarian area of Paris (he has only been there three years, but he goes out among his pagans in the spirit of a missionary), " What proportion of the people do you reach? " And he answered, " Perhaps seven per cent." To those who say there are dangers in the missionary movement one is inclined to answer, Yes, all life is dangerous, but danger is better than death. And the Church of France had the mark of death upon it.

But a better answer was given by Cardinal Suhard. "They are pioneers and pioneers must be allowed to make some mistakes."

One feels, too, the more one studies the movement, that it carries within it the antidotes to its possible errors in the extraordinary variety of its elements and in the width and depth of its range. For here we have not a mere sectional movement but an entire Church becoming missionary. Thus, for instance, the obvious danger of a swing from a too exclusively bourgeois to an exclusively proletarian Church is countered by the remarkable number of bourgeois who are in the movement up to the neck. The rich young man " went away sorrowful " when Christ called him; many since, many today, respond joyfully. Abbé Depierre tells of one who gave up a fortune of ten million francs, keeping for himself and his family only a house and two years' salary, of another who distributed nine-tenths of his property among his employees. Others again have given up good posts to plunge into the insecurity of the proletariat. And it is bourgeois groups who find a large part of the funds to support the various missions, who themselves are living lives of difficulty and often of penury, but who have a new élan of spiritual, liturgical and intellectual life. To equate bourgeois with capitalist is, anyhow, rather absurd. The doctor, the schoolmaster, the lawyer, the small shopkeeper do not merit the scorn so often poured out on the bourgeois. After all, if the middle class has been apt as a whole to cushion life too much, it has also given to the Church some of the finest intellects she has known and some of the highest spirituality. Sainte Thérèse, patron of this as of all missions, was a little girl of the bourgeoisie. You cannot bring an indictment against a class any more than against a nation. The Church is universal vertically as well as horizontally.

Nor can you canonise a class, and I must admit that some of the priests I met do talk as though the proletariat alone had not fallen in Adam. The leaders in the statement referred to above warn of the danger of becoming a priest-workman through " snobisme," and although this is not precisely the same as snobbery in English there is a sense in which the urge to be close to the aristocracy that pervaded the early nineteenth century has been transposed today into a sort of snobbery in reverse. It is mixed up with what the same document calls " secular messianism " which is attached to the Mouvement Ouvrier.

You must always see in the background what sets on fire with anger and misery both the priests and the bourgeois laymen who have plunged into them, the really hideous sufferings that have followed the war in France. A family, itself a cell of the Mission de Paris, was talking to a doctor during the strikes of last year. They were talking in the one room in which the family lives. They sleep on camp beds that are put down at

night and taken up in the morning. There are five in the family
and they often have someone with them who has nowhere else
to sleep. How can they wash, says Doctor Tremolière, or dry
themselves and their clothes in a room where they must cook,
eat, sleep, see their friends, look after their children ? The prices
of clothes and of food are far higher than in England and leaping
up almost day by day. Nobody can live on the ordinary
wage, and the wages are not rising in any proportion with
the prices.

And if there is a simple element in those who, never having
had enough for a human life, believe that contentment and
happiness can be found in these material things that are denied
them, there is on the other hand a deeply serious feeling that
they could create something better than the " established
disorder " in which they are living.

Here are the modern magnificent techniques that should
make man's life easy and here is a life lower than an animal's
on a well-run farm.

The workers have some general ideas of history as seen by a
Marxist, and it is obvious as seen by anybody that the aristocracy has failed and the bourgeoisie has failed. In a kind of
Wellsian rosy glow they see a future in which the proletariat
will succeed where these have failed. The wave of the future
is for them the temporal triumph of the workers. And to it
they attach a very real *mystique* of brotherhood. A *mystique*
is needed, says Godin, to replace a *mystique*. And a Communist
girl said lately to Père Chenu, " The party is magnificent, but
I have learnt that only Christ has life."

There has always been in the Mouvement Ouvrier a Christian
wing: " the J.O.C. isn't as new as all that ", remarked Joseph
Folliet (professor of sociology at the Catholic University of
Lyons). But it is actually only in the last few years that the
consciousness of belonging to the Mouvement Ouvrier has
grown really strong in the J.O.C. Their vocation is, they feel,
to give to the movement a Christian expression of the justice
and fraternity it is seeking.

It seems to me there are two trends in the Catholic movement itself of which one is in some peril of being too much caught up in the Mouvement Ouvrier while the other restores the balance. The one aims at an identification with the workers' movement which shall train up leaders for it. The other, which is more authentically that of Abbé Godin, would at once begin to offer the Catholic *mystique*, is not greatly interested in the training of leaders but rather in the workings of the Holy Spirit in all men, and believes, anyhow, that men must first seek the kingdom of God as well as His justice if these things are to be added unto them. Not that for one moment they dissociate themselves from the struggle for human conditions, for earthly justice, but meanwhile, and in and through that struggle, they believe that Christian communities must be brought into being in the proletariat, the leaven must be put into the dough.

Until this has been done more fully and widely the question will always remain whether the Catholic Movement is strong enough not to be submerged in that of the workers instead of guiding it. The French Church is still suffering because elements in it allowed themselves to be used for the temporal ends first of the ancien régime and lately of Pétainism. It would suffer as much in the future if the attraction now exercised over certain French Catholics by Communism were to become widespread. Godin himself notes as two forms of temporal Messianism: identification with the ruling powers—and revolution. The devil, he says, always tempts the Church as he tempted Christ. " You have come to gather around you the Jewish people. Go to them after the fashion they expect: the Apocalyptic Messiah. Christ as man must have desired success. There was the conflict: the Jews were looking for a leader, a temporal Messiah.

" To make an alliance with the devil instead of fighting him: because the devil is stronger than we are.

" Who realises the depth of suffering with which Christ always took God's side against Satan?

" *Father if it be possible.*"

The quotation is from Abbé Godin's spiritual notes which came into my hands at this point, where I found this awareness of a danger for the Church today, shown in figure by the temptations of Our Lord. The last temptation " cannot have been explicit. The devil isn't such a fool. The Gospel wants to show us that the third is the natural outcome of the first two."

It requires the intensity of prayer and meditation with which Godin balanced his immense activities, it requires what he has called the " mystic nights " of an apostle who puts all into God's hands for the safeguarding of the transcendence of the Church in a period in which her immanence in the world of men has to be so strongly asserted. Catholics today are reacting against a fear of human life that made religion almost a soul without a body; no one more strongly than Godin demanded a constant incarnation of the mystical Christ in the world of today, but no one insisted more strongly on the transcendent, on the supernatural.

" Man must act in everything as a being created to know and love God and to rise up to life with the Trinity " (Lisieux notes).

Then too, while the Mouvement Ouvrier has many historic pages over which the Christian worker can grow enthusiastic, the Marxist vision of history grows pale when set beside that great march of God with man shown in the Bible and in the history of the Catholic Church.

At the Mission de France, now seven years old, this has been fully realised and a new direction has been given to the seminary studies, which stresses especially history and scripture. The students themselves in a striking paper describe their preparation for the Mission, which they see as the " Church's effort to get loose from the civilisation that is passing away and to insert Herself as a living ferment into that new civilisation which, apart from Her, is in danger of being swallowed up by paganism."

They go on to describe their own preparation:

" The Bible is not only our great textbook: it is also our great book of spirituality: it is inexhaustible. Supremely we have learnt from it

—that Christianity is not in the first place a doctrine or a system, but a life: the concrete story of the living contacts of man with a God who became man to teach us to live our human life in a divine way;

—that we are caught up into a mighty march of history, the economy of which Saint Paul speaks, a movement guided by God towards the building of the heavenly Jerusalem, which He will direct for good despite the opposition of men;

—that our own best method of active collaboration with this immense plan of God's is to join ourselves to those poor whom God has always loved to make use of, of whom the perfect example is the Virgin Mary.

" Above all, we have learnt that our priesthood is itself a profound source of wealth. Incorporated into the Church, made one with all those—the hierarchy, the clergy and the laity responsible like ourselves, each one in his order, for the salvation of the world—the priesthood constitutes us mediators building a bridge between God and man, obliged like the Word Incarnate to be in closest contact with men and with God. Our mediation should, like Christ's, be fulfilled by a redemptive labour that links us intimately with the sufferings and sins of men. This priestly life is fed and centred in the Divine Office, prayer of the entire Church, offered in the name of all mankind, in the sacraments which give birth to God's life in us and in our brethren: above all in the Mass, the very heart of the Church, whereby Jesus Christ is made present through us.

.   .   .   .

" An ever deepening approach to the Christian Message leads us to a more synthetic grasp of the content of divine revelation, bringing together the various aspects of doctrine and reassembling theological treatises that are sometimes too widely separated. Especially the study of the theological virtues and of morality is replaced in its close dependence on dogma.

" We aim at grasping the Message through discovering the Christian fact revealed in the story of God's chosen people and of the Church. Great importance is attached to revelation through history. The first three years are devoted (besides philosophy) to the study of the Bible and of God's interventions in the world—to the theology of the New Testament and the history of the Church which casts light on the development of the Christian fact. Dogmatic theology spread over the last two years then enables us to go over revelation again as a whole.

" Our study is never pursued apart from its apostolic end. Pastoral conclusions introduced at the end of theological treatises are not enough. We all try through our studies to keep in touch with life, and this attempt forces us to make a serious analysis of the human element. It is, in fact, a reshaping within us of the form of the message that we are trying to achieve by studying both God's action in the world and human life.

. . . . .

" This type of intellectual effort appears to us to be an indispensable preparation for missionary work."

A WIDE vision of the work to be done and the spirit of its doing is not limited to the Missions de France, de Paris, de Marseille, etc. Another document, issued by them and by Catholic Action chaplains, declares that these movements must not be treated as alternatives, but as complementary one of the other. They must be fulfilled and completed in their relation to the parish —"the great fundamental reality," Father Loew calls it. We must, he says, " bring back the youth, the joy, the dynamism of the parish; all other efforts will be broken by this failure."

Increasingly the parish stands out as the solution to almost every question asked in these pages.

Is the formula " go to the people " correct, asks Cardinal Saliège—or do we not need to complete it by adding, " go to the bourgeois ", " go to the student "? In every class there are pagans to be sought out, and each class would bring its own share of qualities to the common stock. A young " prolo " in the stage that Godin would have called the catechumenate remarked to a friend of mine: " I don't go to that bourgeois Mass, only to Father So-and-so's." Parishes within a parish for national or other special groups are only permitted by Canon Law for a time under special circumstances. The Church in the factory, the Church in the home, must depend upon, be in contact with its parish, become a mission sent out by it. The parish remains the home and the centre for all her children who realise their unity in the House of their Father. If the bourgeois Catholic failed to seek the proletarian, the proletarian must not in turn excommunicate the bourgeois. Human beings are the stuff in which the Church works: and they are apt to be exceedingly human. In nothing do they show it more than in canonising their own views and declaring them the views of the Church. An acute critic[1] has pointed out the danger that human communities, even when being turned into Christian communities, may be united chiefly by a warm feeling arising more from ideas shared in common and natural affections than from divine grace. The great danger of the French Church does appear to be the political one: if the new movement is halted it will almost certainly be for political reasons. And the devil is very clever in the matter: for each side has hold of some important truths neglected by the other.

During the 1947 strikes Dr. Tremolière was visiting two of his patients: a director and a workman, one furiously against, the other furiously for, the strike. The one looked *only* at the perilous condition of his industry, the other *only* at the sufferings of the men. And the doctor concluded, " Were I the director I should be against, were I the worker I should be for the strike."

On a larger scale the Conservative Catholics in France see clearly the awful sufferings of Rumanians, Poles and others under Russia. They see the peril of France itself and they blame the leftists who toy with Communism. The leftists see clearly the sufferings of the workers and blame the Conservatives for ignoring them. And both are right. The trouble is that everyone in France does everything fiercely, above all the intellectuals, which makes it more than difficult for Catholics to fill their ideal role of making a synthesis. They above all should help the warring elements each to see the truth in the other's attitude. Alas, for the most part, they are not doing it.

But indirectly the missionary parish, the missionary movement itself, is beginning the task of reconciliation. For it is bringing Catholics together who can through their religion prescind from their natural political standpoints in favour of greater and more vitally interesting topics. I dined in a workman's house with three seminarians from the Mission de France, one young ex-seminarian who was a peasant turned

[1] Zacharie Serrand, in the *Vie Intellectuelle*, Oct. 1945.

teacher, a doctor, a Jocist. Not a word of politics was spoken: we talked of Abbé Godin first, of ways of approach to pagans, of the different methods needed for gaining an entry to the mind of the intellectual or of the simple, of the problem of birth control in the slums of Paris. We talked of the seminary training at Lisieux. One of the young men was in the midst of his " stade " as a worker and he confessed frankly his disappointment at the selfishness he had often found where he had expected brotherhood. An extraordinary sense of reality pervaded the evening: it began with our hostess cooking the dinner while a seminarian coaxed one child to eat and the father put the other to bed. The whole flat was two tiny rooms: by shutting the doors we were just able to sit round the table—provided nobody moved. Late into the night we talked—and here was surely material for the authentic unity into which the ideal parish can bring all men. " There is now neither Jew nor Gentile, neither bond nor free, but all are one in Christ." The parish should be the truest expression of that unity.

It can hardly be doubted that the chief weakening of the missionary movement lies outside it—in the number of parishes not yet caught up in it.

I have been lately staying near one of these. The Church was depressing beyond words: a chaisière noisily collecting her francs for the chairs all through Mass, a Suisse banging on the floor as a priest followed him audibly requesting " le denier du culte ". One wondered what any pagan would feel who had been told how sacred the Mass is held by Catholics: it was literally what Abbé Michonneau has called " the clink of money round the altar ". In the distance the priest murmuring so low that even with a missal it was impossible to discover what Mass he was saying, an old woman responding in a hushed voice. Outside the church an immense notice announced the music at Sunday's High Mass exactly like a concert programme. It was all worlds away from the magnificent vistas opened by the liturgical reviews (the *Maison-Dieu*, *Art Sacré*, *Les Albums*

Liturgiques, etc.) and still more by such books as *Paroisse Communauté Missionaire.* These have built up for me a vision that is being shaped into a reality today in very many French parishes. The life of these new parishes is orientated in a missionary direction. Catholic families are asked regularly to invite their unbelieving friends to meet their priest, who will then answer any questions they like to put to him. These meetings are an immense success: each Catholic family is proud when its turn comes, the others happy to be invited. As many as twenty-five are squeezed into a small house and discussions on such subjects as eternity, pain and the love of God, the purpose of man's life, will go on as long as the curé wishes to prolong them. Abbé Lorenzo of the Mission de France, as well as Abbé Michonneau, thinks of this as one of the most useful of their activities. Is it not, says Abbé Michonneau, the primitive apostolate, that of the apostles themselves? If persecution swept all the rest away that would still be left us. And it is the best.

" I have prepared a series of sermons," says a country curé, " for the people who only come to church on the great feasts. I have four chances a year of instructing them and I know these sermons are followed closely."

Some of the pagans met in Catholic houses will come to the church on business—and what is the business that brings them? " Circumstances that usually lead to heart-to-heart talks: a marriage, a funeral, a First Communion, the home, immortality, the child; the biggest questions, the things that leave no one indifferent. What splendid opportunities to speak as a priest, to open a heart and show it horizons never glimpsed before. How can we be so idiotic as to be dry and practical at such times when we might be human and apostolic? "[1]

Funerals, the giving of the Sacraments, are all made an occasion for reaching a world that only at such times becomes readily accessible. One country priest gets the whole village together at the house the night before a funeral, and between

[1] *Paroisse Communauté Missionaire, p.* 186-7.

decades of the rosary explains to them the Mass for the Dead.
" These evenings are an immense success." Another prepares
a special sermon for each wedding, preaches it in the presence
of all the young people, the *jeunes foyers* of the future, and then
writes it out with a special dedication and gives it to the bride.
" I have already had multiple proof that many of the brides
begin to dream of a married life based on the ideals they have
so often heard set forth."

To create opportunities for the direct apostolate, most
missionary curés hold that a considerable work of demolition
is called for. For one thing they feel that, while Catholics
should realise, and indeed be made to appreciate, the duty of
supporting their clergy, the pagan world is alienated by " the
clink of money round the altar ". Hence in most of these
parishes a collection is made on Sunday morning only, payment
for chairs suppressed or asked only every three months of the
" regulars ". The various classes of weddings and funerals are
abolished so that the poorest feel that the services of the church
are fully at their disposal: this is facilitated by the fact that in
most of these churches congregational singing is the rule.
Thus the man with most friends has the biggest congregation
and the " best " Mass. The financial result of this policy was
neatly summed up by Père Chenu. " If a priest keeps his parish
alive, the parish will keep him alive."

One question much discussed brings out the contrast
between the nature of missionary work in France and in the
Anglo-Saxon countries. With us it is normal that a child is
baptised because its parents are Catholics and intend to bring
it up one. But in France a baptism may well be the merest
gesture on the part of the parents—to please a grandmother, or
because " it's always been done in our family. It won't hurt
him. It may even come in handy if he wants a church marriage
later ". Country curés for the most part know they will have
the child at least up to his Solemn First Communion. But in the
big towns it is becoming increasingly customary for the priest
to ask of the parents as a condition of baptism a promise to

bring the child up a Catholic. The hour for baptisms is set before or after Sunday High Mass and the ceremony is invested with all possible solemnity—that the parish may receive its new member joyfully and may bear witness to the parents' promise that he will be brought up a member of the flock.

A similar situation arises with marriages. Where we should have a dispensation and a mixed marriage, the French Church has for years assumed the Catholicity of all who have been baptised and has often bestowed baptism on one of the parties if the other wanted a religious ceremony. Many priests today are reacting against this. They do not believe that the best way of converting a pagan is to pretend that he is already a Catholic. And, too, the moral question has come much more to the fore than a few years back. Do the couple really intend to make a Christian marriage with all that it involves? Or do they look on birth control as normal and divorce as a way out should the marriage turn out a failure? The tendency is on the increase to probe into these questions, to make them, if possible, realise what Christian marriage means, but to refuse a religious ceremony to those who are determined on a non-Christian contract that could be made equally well in a registry office.

Even with Christians there are almost certain to be some members of the family outside the Church, and one curé told me that he makes of every marriage, baptism and funeral an occasion to make contact with these by visits to the house.

Probably by now readers will be asking how the overdriven priests in the large cities can possibly find time for all this extra work. And Abbé Michonneau answers this question by an account of the largely useless activities that he has swept out of his parish to make room for the direct apostolate. Boys' clubs that did little but keep their members out of mischief for a few hours, the parish cinema which had hardly a Catholic picture to show but simply chose out the least objectionable secular pictures. Catholic boxing? says the Abbé. Catholic football? Catholic billiards? Are we going to segregate our boys so thoroughly that we must build Catholic swimming pools, and purchase a Catholic mountain? Year after year we have said, We have the children, so the next generation is ours, and life has given the lie to these assertions. By all our emphasis on good works among the young " we have not succeeded in creating Christian men and women ".

What he would keep and fortify is Catholic Action: for this can make even boys and girls into apostles; trying to " put the whole of Christianity into the whole of life ", trying to fulfil Canon Cardijn's aim by thinking first of " those who do not belong to us ".

Cardinal Saliège gives a chief reason why it is possible for Catholic Action to do a greater thing than any ordinary parochial " good work ". Good works demand free time and modern life leaves most people little or no time free from the exigencies of professional and family life. " Apostles in their free time? No, for they have none. Apostles all the time? Yes, for they are apostles in their professions, in their families, in their every field of activity ".[1]

This means of necessity that much of their work cannot be parochial: the missionary parish priest accepts this fact. It is the task of groups, strongly federated, with priests set aside for the purpose, to train up Catholic leaders who shall take their part in the Mouvement Ouvrier and in the whole life of the country.[2]

But a wise parish priest can also perhaps more than anyone understand and help to implement the apparent paradox of Catholic Action—that in it the priest is everything and he is nothing. If missionary Catholic Action has to go outside the parish it begins inside. It is, or can be, the sharp point of penetration into the pagan world; it is or can be a powerful missionary element of the parish. Abbé Michonneau points out that while there were failures when the curé turned his Jocists into a mere parochial group there might be greater

[1] *Les Menus Propos de Cardinal Saliège*, VII, p. 43.
[2] A most interesting light is cast on all this by the March-April 1948 number of *Masses Ouvrières* with its account of Catholic Action in last year's strikes.

failures if he left them unguided. Their aim must be "the supernatural first. We want Christ everywhere. Charity, justice and the other social virtues should come forth from Christ living in His militants who are His members. If this order is reversed there is a risk of not getting beyond the merely human, the missionary apostolate will not be carried on ".

Abbé Michonneau declares that he wants " a Christianity that runs the streets ". Not afraid of encountering the pagan world, his boys and girls say proudly, " We Christians ", as they boast a little, perhaps, of the works carried out on their holidays: helping a poor woman, visiting a sick child, chopping wood for an old man. Their parents inspire these acts as well as the priests. For most of the directly charitable work of the parish is handed over to a laity well fitted to cope, while the very teaching of the Catechism comes to the children with a missionary slant. They know they have something to give to the little pagans they meet in the streets and playgrounds. One child proudly produced a recruit at the catechism class. " I baptised her myself at the street pump. Her mother wouldn't have allowed it."

A little further instruction for the young apostle was certainly indicated—but the general trend was sound enough. It is grand not to be " defending " the Church, but only longing to offer Her graces to all. Teaching given in the midst of life, life does not destroy.

Not too much perhaps, but certainly a wrong stress had been laid on " the children "; now the stress is on the family. All Catholic families must be missionary—and they can only give what they have got, they can only teach what they themselves understand. Missionary parishes emphasise specially an adult Christian education. The Mouvement Populaire des Familles has its own newspaper, the *Editions Ouvrières* have an admirable monthly, *Masses Ouvrières*; supremely there are the *Albums Liturgiques*; for the more educated the Catholic periodicals of today are past counting.

But above all, for this profound education and preparation for the apostolate the Missionary Church stresses the liturgy and the sermon.

This is the point at which the great theological and liturgical movements of today may be said to flow into and complete the missionary movement, and to give the answer to some of Abbé Godin's most poignant questions.

Must the priest's culture really divide him from his flock? Must the liturgy remain a preserve for the archaeologist? The Mission de France has answered by showing that it is not the ideas but the technical language in which theology has long been taught that forms the barrier. And they have begun to teach their students how to break this barrier down.

Such periodicals as *Art Sacré*, *Albums Liturgiques* and, above all, the *Maison Dieu*, show us something of the historical side: how this barrier was erected, not in the great ages of the Church, but in the age of scholastic and liturgical decadence.

Cardinal Saliège, referring to the bad period which (we hope) is passing away, remarks, " Many people imagine that a sermon is full of doctrine when it abounds in abstract terms that nobody can understand." Thus La Bruyère had written in *Les Caractères* that a man must know a prodigious amount to be able to preach so badly. But, says Cardinal Saliège, " a sermon can be made up of doctrine without thereby becoming hard to understand ".

Dom Leclerq quotes these words in an issue of the *Maison Dieu* on the parish. He is writing of the sermon, as it was conceived in the early Church and in the Middle Ages, as the completion of the work of the liturgy in teaching the fullness of revelation to the whole people:

" To preach the great mysteries of salvation to the simple faithful you must know the difficult theological expressions, and the arduous task of the preacher is to set out in terms understandable by everybody the ideas he has first thought out in scholastic terminology. . . . In the normal life of the Church theology is the preparation for fruitful preaching and this helps us to understand the purpose and the meaning of all the theological energy poured out in the Middle Ages. . . ."

The liturgy is itself doctrinal, revealing to the intellect those mysteries accomplished through it for the soul. But the sermon is vital if the ordinary man is to learn the full meaning of his prayers and of the Sacraments he receives. In the thirteenth century " no gulf separated the pulpit from the school. Preachers were often doctors: the sermons are fed on doctrine drawn like scholastic theology from the sources of Christian tradition especially Holy Scripture. But instead of being expressed in abstract analogies and philosophic concepts this teaching is translated into comparisons drawn from the categories of thought with which the people were familiar . . . the concrete expression of a theology adapted to listeners who are not theologians: if it makes concessions to the popular imagination it sacrifices nothing of the essentials of Christian teaching.

" And it is noteworthy that the theological decadence that followed the golden age of scholasticism coincided with decadence in preaching, shown by the abandonment of the elements that had made it vital in the thirteenth century: its being treated as part of the liturgy, its biblical inspiration, its search for simplicity ".

This article is called " The Sermon a Liturgical Act ", and while the training at Lisieux helps to bring back the old simplicity of the sermon, the general missionary trend is restoring it to its place of honour in the liturgy. The great event in a popular parish is a Sunday High Mass in which the congregation participate and of which the sermon (necessarily short) is an integral part. Nor is the decree of the Council of Trent forgotten, that the meaning of Mass should frequently be explained to the people. I met a seminarian from Lisieux who declared that he had not only had a Catholic education, but had been right through his junior seminary without understanding what the Mass was, and I remember in England a liturgiologist who told me indignantly, " Most Catholics just

think of Mass as machinery for producing Holy Communion."
Today's missionary Catholicism centres on the understanding
of the Mass.

In an interesting article Père Roguet discusses the nature
and results of what has been christened para-liturgy. He defines
it as " a manifestation which without being actually liturgical
is related to the liturgy, formed in a liturgical style, and plays
the part of a servant in relation to the liturgy proper ". The
term came in at the opening of the Centre of Pastoral Liturgy
in 1943.

Abbé Michonneau stresses a use of para-liturgy designed
mainly for unbelievers. It frequently takes the form of a
repetition in the evening and in the vernacular (especially in
Holy Week, at Easter and the other great feasts) of part of the
ceremonies celebrated for believers in Latin in the morning.
For instance, he publishes a version of the Reproaches and of
other parts of the Holy Week Services in French. Another form
of " para-liturgy " is spectacular—the showing of a scene from
the Passion, set on a stage in the Church, or again a slow
exhibition of the ceremonies of Mass accompanied by an
explanation of them. I found variety of opinion as to the
value of these methods which are well summarised by Père
Roguet (*Art Sacré*, August–September 1947).

But that the liturgy itself should be alive, should be pastoral,
is the great aim of the movement as a whole. The dialogue Mass
is very popular, made only, as the Pope orders, of less importance than the parochial Sunday High Mass.

In France Latin singing by the congregation had never
been wholly lost (witness the French pilgrims at Lourdes),
but in the new wave of popular liturgy it has taken on a wider
extent, a deeper significance.

Then, too, many Order priests, many Catholic Action leaders,
make a special point of reviving the Faith in a pagan area
through the ceremonies of Holy Week carried out as fully and
as popularly as possible. Father Henri Perrin, S.J., has done
much of this, going into various villages for Holy Week with

a group of boys to help the parish priest. Father Humbert, O.P., gives a fascinating description of his experiences at a church where he went several years in succession.

In a chapel set aside for Catholic Action groups he began on Palm Sunday, the year the Jocist Missal was published, to have the Passion read in French. A Rover, a Jocist and a Jécist represented respectively the narrator, the crowd and Our Lord. The next year he had ten young men of whom five, very carefully trained, spoke as the crowd. He invited the parish priest to be present who begged that in future the church should be used. Increasing the crowd to twenty, Father Humbert complied. "A shudder went through the congregation as twenty men's voices cried, 'Crucify Him'."

Soon after this one of the Jocists, who had heard the singing of the Passion in a monastery, remarked, "It was magnificent, but I didn't understand the Latin, and there was only one man for the voice of the people." This phrase, "the voice of the people", stayed in Father Humbert's mind. After all, he thought, why should not the people themselves utter the voice of the people?

So in 1944 on Palm Sunday at a Mass dialogued in Latin but with the Proper read in French he arranged besides his chief readers: Christ, the narrator, etc., and two trained groups representing the friends and the enemies of Our Lord, that on every seat should be placed a book indicating in large letters the words uttered by the crowd and the manner of speaking them.

"The effect," he says, "was overwhelming. When the whole church cried out, 'Take Him away. Crucify Him', it was horrifying."

Never before had he himself realised the grief, the loneliness, of Christ when not the rulers alone but the entire people were unleashed against Him.

"When I shouted 'Crucify Him'," men, women and boys told Father Humbert, "I realised it was my sins that were shouting it." And an actor-manager who had come to look on wrote afterwards, " I wish I had the faith to be able to act in that drama."[1]

For an instant he had seen as the supreme drama of human life this manifestation of the God-Man, the true Messiah accomplishing the redemption of man through the agony of the Cross, the triumph of the Resurrection, the glory of the Ascension: Christ the King in Whom all things must be restored.

For if false Messianism is a danger for the world today it is the mission of Christ's priest to bring to it Christ Himself, the true Messiah. This mission it was the aim of Godin's life to rediscover for those who perhaps had forgotten, in what he called the " established official " view of the priesthood, their higher and holier office " as evangelist and prophet—he who speaks in the name of God."

" Faith in the fruitfulness of our priesthood will drive out the official. To escape from officialism we must be driven by the love of God, the value of everything else is only relative."

It was felt by the priests who knew him most intimately that Godin's mission to them was no less, might indeed be more significant even, than his mission to his boys and girls. To Jocists he had shown the beauty of a Christian marriage, of an unfailing courage in parenthood, of a sanctification of human life through one social sacrament. For himself and his fellow priests he was ever meditating on the significance of the other. And characteristically he told his young couples, " God says, ' I don't care much for old bachelors '," and commented in his notes that celibacy, unless it raises a man higher than his fellows, will sink him lower. For the service of a family brings with it much self-sacrifice. But not so much as a fully lived priestly vocation. " Himself an awakener of divine life, the priest must believe in it, be a man of prayer and sacrifice, a mediator, a prolongation of Christ, a prophet praying and offering himself."

[1] *La Maison Dieu*, No. 8, pp. 103-4.

" The priest is a living sacrament, a source of life throughout his life." To this thought he returns again and again. " The presence of the priest is a source of grace. We are living sacraments. There is a mysticism of action in the priesthood, for the Sacrament of Holy Orders is in us abidingly. We have developed the idea of an established clergy, let us rediscover together the *mystique* of our priesthood: a shared *mystique.*"

" We are too much inclined to put up fences. The great safeguard of our priestly life is to grow towards a total priesthood."

" Direction should mean making contact with a power station."

The priest must be both a mystic dwelling with God and a man in the midst of men. He must go out and cry the Gospels from the housetops. The world will always have a religion true or false.

In *France, Pays de Mission?* Godin had stressed this absolute necessity for man of some sort of religion: in their discussions the missionary priests spoke of a secular messianism—no longer of race and blood like that of Hitler or his French prototypes but of class—arising to fulfil that need. But the true Messiah Christ is always there, hiddenly acting through the men He has chosen. If nothing will replace a false *mystique* except a true *mystique*, none but Christ can drive out Antichrist.

The world always needs evangelising afresh. Yet too the priest must constantly by his exercises of piety be " keeping company with God " (here he uses the same expression—*fréquentation*—that is used for a boy and girl going out together).

The Christian man and girl keep company, they have "belles fiançailles" as Godin taught them, for their personal sanctification, for the children to come, for their life together in the Mystical Body of Christ. The priest " keeping company with God " is supremely fulfilling his essential office in that Body.

" A thought has struck me," writes Godin, " saying the breviary is an essentially priestly occupation. All Christians who have forgotten their baptism, all the young workers who have to be won back: I can make them all pray, I do make them all pray when as a Christian I recite my breviary.

" When I make them pray badly that's hardly the way to convert them. Work [for souls] is priestly of its essence. To live the divine in man, to lift the human to God. Well, the breviary is part of that. It is action for the sake of souls.

" I must remember when I say my office that I am making the whole Church pray."

If this is true of the Office, how much more of the Mass.

" The priest who wants to say Mass well must gather into himself all the suffering of humanity: their needs, their longings, their hopes. He must be the priest of humanity, understanding it to the depths.

" The more fully the priest is a man, the more he becomes God. Above all in Holy Communion.

" He communicates in the name of the whole human race but especially those who are committed to his care.

" After Mass my action becomes the action of Christ."

And again:

" Priestly prayer, a rightly directed ministry, mean that the priest is closely welded with men, has taken them all in charge, but especially some one section.

" The priest must feel the need of God for himself and for others: when I receive Communion I desire to unite Christ with all men (memento of the living, priest who says the names as he gives Communion). When I give Communion I am giving them Christ."

If France be indeed a missionary land, it is certainly today a land of missionaries. And the world witnesses this in the great and vital assemblies for liturgical, social, theological discussions and manifestations wherein the oldest of institutions gives proof of its eternal youth.

Just as the separate movements—missions, Catholic Action, liturgical and social groups flow into the parish, so are all the parishes joined in a wider unity. Let us end this utterly inadequate sketch of the beginnings of a great movement with the meeting of parishes in the Stadium at Colombes in 1946.

It was only the Paris area, yet, as priest after priest passed by, leading his own congregation into the arena, witnesses were overwhelmed with the sense of the unity in catholicity of the Church thus represented.

Two hundred parish priests at two hundred altars said Mass together. A hundred thousand worshippers cried together: " Amen ", " Et cum spiritu tuo ", and answered the " Sursum corda " of the celebrants with " Habemus ad Dominum ". At one same moment two hundred voices pronounced the words of consecration, a hundred thousand worshippers were still and silent in adoration. Each priest gave communion at his own altar to his own parishioners, and then once more a hundred thousand voices took up the *Pange Lingua*, the *Tantum Ergo* and the *Magnificat*, giving thanks to God for all His graces and His great glory in the Mass.

I AM PUTTING these two together because the most important of my sources lie in the minds of men or in manuscripts which have been most kindly lent to me.

I owe most of all to conversations: with Abbé Hollande and Abbé Daniel of the Mission de Paris, with Père Chenu, Père Travers and Père Berger, O.P., Père Perrin, S.J., Abbé Lorenzo of the Mission de France, Dr. Tremolière, Marcel Müller, André and Madeleine Huot, Roger Beaunez and a host of others in France, with Father Langdale of the Young Christian Workers and Michael Derrick in England.

Of Abbé Godin's unpublished writings the most important are: *Pensées de chaque Jour* and *Retraites* which run from his seminary days down to somewhere near the end of his life, *Plans de Récollection* with questionnaires for his Jeunes Foyers, and finally the big folder of notes and outlines for the meetings and retreat which launched the Mission de Paris.

Other unpublished documents are *La Mission de Paris*, given me by Abbé Hollande, *Rapport de Mission* by Fathers André and Rogatien (Capuchins), *La Déchristianisation en France—Les Orientations de l'Apostolat—La Mission de France*, written by a group of Lisieux students, *Réunion des Religieux missionaires ouvriers*, Jan. 1948.

Of pamphlets there are two editions of Canon Augros' *Mission de France*, one published in 1941, the other in 1945, which together give an excellent idea of the progress of the Mission from its beginnings. Then there is the *Mission de France Féminine* of 1947; and in the same year a sort of super-leaflet with a map of France and a year by year record of progress.

Turning to books there is a fairly solid list which is still probably incomplete.

FOR PART I

Témoignages sur l'Abbé Godin—Les Editions ouvrières.

Un Homme Providentiel: L'Abbé Godin—P. GLORIEUX—Bonne Presse.

Le Levain dans la pâte—HENRI GODIN—Les Editions ouvrières.

Le Christ sur la Ligne Maginot—HENRI GODIN—Les Editions ouvrières.

Retraites et Récollections—HENRI GODIN—Les Editions ouvrières.

Avec le Christ—*Missel de Formule Moderne*—HENRI GODIN—Les Editions ouvrières.

Jeunesse qui reconstruit—ed. HENRI GODIN—Les Editions ouvrières.

Jeunesse qui s'épanouit—ed. HENRI GODIN—Les Editions ouvrières.

"Ceux que tu m'as donnés"—(par l'Equipe)—Les Editions ouvrières.

Restoring All Things—JOHN FITZSIMMONS and PAUL McGUIRE—Sheed and Ward.

Témoignages sur l'Amour—DR. JOUVENROUX—Les Editions ouvrières.

FOR PART III

Paroisse Communauté missionaire—Abbé MICHONNEAU—Ed. du Cerf. (being translated under title, *Revolution in a City Parish*—Blackfriars Press).

Communauté Paroissiale et liturgique—H. Ch. CHÉRY, O.P.—Ed. du Cerf.

Problèmes missionaires de la France rurale—F. BOULARD avec la collaboration de A. ACHARD et H. J. EMERARD (2 vols.)—Ed. du Cerf.

Les "Menus Propos" du Cardinal Saliège, especially No. VII—L'équipe d'Action. Also his *Temps present et l'Action Catholique*—Ed. ouvrières.

Les Dockers de Marseille and *En Mission prolétarienne*—M. R. LOEW, O.P.—Economie et Humanisme.

Priest Workman in Germany—HENRI PERRIN—Sheed and Ward.

The Priest in a Changing World—ROBERT KOTHEN—Sheed and Ward.

Prison et Déportation—Mgr. GABRIEL PIQUET—Ed. Spes.

Les trois Tentations de l'Apostolat moderne—HENRI DUMERY—Ed. du Cerf.

Finally we have constant accounts in periodical literature: the following magazines carry significant articles almost month by month:

La Maison Dieu (Cahiers de Pastorale Liturgiques), Ed. du Cerf—especially No. 8.

La Vie Intellectuelle, especially Oct. 1945 and Jan. 1948.

La Vie Spirituelle, especially Supplement No. 5, May 1948, *Adaptations de la Vie religieuse*.

Albums Liturgiques: Fêtes et Saisons, Ed. du Cerf.

Masses Ouvrières, Editions Ouvrières.

L'Art Sacré, Ed. du Cerf.

Esprit, especially Aug.–Sept. 1946.